## About the author

Tony Buzan, inventor of the now world-famous Mind Maps®, has achieved an astonishing series of accomplishments.

- The world's leading author on the brain and learning with over 80 authored and co-authored books to date and with sales totalling three million and accelerating!
- The world's top lecturer on the brain and learning. The 'Mind Magician', as Tony Buzan has increasingly become known, has lectured to audiences ranging from five-year-old children through disadvantaged students to first-class Oxbridge graduates, to the world's top business directors, and to the leading organisations and governments.
- Founder of the World Memory Championships.
- Founder of the World Speed Reading Championships.
- Black belt in the martial arts.
- Buzan's books and other products have achieved massive success in more than 100 countries and 30 languages, generating revenues in excess of £100 million.
- Inventor of Mind Maps®, the thinking tool described as 'the Swiss army knife of the brain', now used by over 250 million people worldwide.
- Editor, the international journal of MENSA (the high IQ society) from 1968–1971.
- International business consultant to major multinationals including: BP, Barclays International, General Motors, Walt Disney, Oracle, Microsoft, HSBC, British Telecom, IBM, British Airways, etc.
- Consultant and adviser to governments and government organisations including: England, Singapore, Mexico, Australia, the Gulf States and Liechtenstein.
- Olympic Coach.
- Originator of the concepts of Radiant Thinking and Mental Literacy.
- Prize-winning poet.
- Prize-winning athlete.
- A global media personality, having appeared on over 100 hours of national and global television, and over 1000 hours of national and international radio. Has been seen and heard by an estimated three billion-plus people!

D1369122

# Also by Tony Buzan

## Books

The Mind Set:

Use Your Head
Use Your Memory
The Speed Reading Book
The Mind Map Book
The Illustrated Mind Map Book

Embracing Change

Buzan Bites:

Brilliant Memory
Mind Mapping
Speed Reading

Get Ahead
Brain S£11
Super Sell
BrainSmart Leader
Sales Genius
Mind Maps in Medicine
The Brain Book
Brain Training
Lessons from the Art of Juggling
Buzan's Book of Mental World Records
Man Versus Machine
Synapsia (Individual)
Synapsia (89–99 complete set)
The Younger Tongue
Brain Power for Kids
Teach Yourself Revision Guides
(GCSE level in 17 subjects)

Teach Yourself Revision Guides
(A level in 8 subjects)

Teach Yourself Literature Guides
(22 titles)

How to Mind Map
The Power of Social Intelligence
The Power of Verbal Intelligence
Head Strong
The Power of Creative Intelligence
Head First
Mind Maps for Kids

## Video tapes

Learning with Lana
Developing Family Genius
Get Ahead
If at First . . .
Mindpower

## Audio tapes

Use Your Head

Buzan On . . .

The Brain
Memory
Thinking & Creativity
Success
Reading
Mind & Body
Mind Mapping

Mind Mapping Natural Genius
The Genius Formula
Brain S£ll

## Other products

Brain Club – Home Study Plan
Body & Soul Poster (Limited Edition)
Desiderata Reconsidered
Universal Personal Organiser
Mind Map Kit

## Software

Mind Manager (CD-ROM)
Mind Manager (Trial CD-ROM)
Mastering Memory
(Computer Software & Manual)

# Master Your Memory

## Tony Buzan

**B** **B** **C** ACTIVE

153.1      Q      47919

# Dedicated to my dear friends in the Brain Clubs and Buzan Centres

## External Editor-in-chief: Vanda North
### Special Consultants: Dr Susan Whiting, GMM
### Grandmaster Raymond Keene, OBE

Published by Educational Publishers LLP trading as BBC Active
Edinburgh Gate, Harlow, Essex, CM20 2JE, England

Copyright Tony Buzan 1974, 1982, 1989, 1995, 2000, 2003, 2006

BBC logo © BBC 1996. BBC and BBC ACTIVE are trademarks of the British Broadcasting Corporation

First published in 1988
Revised and updated 1989, 1998, 2000, 2003
This edition published in 2006

The right of Tony Buzan to be identified as author of this Work has been asserted by him/her in accordance with the Copyright, Designs and Patents Act, 1988..

All rights reserved. No part of this publication may be reproduced, stored in a retrieval system or transmitted in any form or by any means electronic, mechanical, photocopying, recording, or otherwise, without either the prior written permission of the publishers and copyright owners or a licence permitting restricted copying in the United Kingdom issued by the Copyright Licensing Agency Ltd, 90 Tottenham Court Road, London W1T 4LP.

ISBN 1406610224

Mind Map® is a registered trademark of the Buzan Organisation Limited 1990
Mental Literacy® is a registered trademark of the Buzan Organisation Limited 1994
Radiant Thinking® is a registered trademark of the Buzan Organisation Limited 1994
Buzan™ is a trademark of the Buzan Organization Limited 2006

Series design by Ben Cracknell Studios
Illustrations by Alan Burton and Ben Cracknell

Commissioning Editor: Emma Shackleton
Project Editors: Sarah Lavelle and Julia Charles

Set in Meridien
Printed and bound by Ashford Colour Press, UK

The Publisher's policy is to use paper manufactured from sustainable forests.

# Contents

# Appreciation

My heart- and mind-felt thanks to the following for their masterful and memorable performances: to Dr Susan Whiting, Grandmaster of Memory and four-times Women's World Memory Champion, for her creative and unceasing efforts in helping me to refine SEM$^3$, in helping others understand, appreciate and use it, and for being the current reigning 'SEM$^3$ Champion'!; to Vanda North, my External Editor-in-Chief, for her dedication and support of the concept and for her utter and joyful dedication to the vision of a Mentally Literate Planet; to International Chess and Mind Sports Grandmaster Raymond Keene, OBE, for his ground-breaking work on the identification and ranking of genius, and for his cogent insights into the body of Shakespeare's works; to Memory Grandmaster Ian Docherty for his on-going help with the development of SEM$^3$ and for his Master Mind Map, which inspired the Mind Maps you will find in this book; to the wonderful artists Lorraine Gill and Christopher Hedley-Dent for their help in educating me in the appreciation of art and their intensive research support for 'the Artists' section of this book; to my Personal Assistant Lesley Bias who kept all other systems running immaculately while also overseeing the production of this manuscript; to my dear mother, Jean Buzan, whose 'eagle editorial eye' caught over twenty-five errors in the 'finished manuscript'; to my Research Assistant and computer-whiz Susanne Pumpin who gathered much invaluable information and who transferred the bulk of the information in this book from my brain to her computer's brain!; to Dominic O'Brien, six-time and dawn of millennium reigning World Memory Champion, for manifesting everything that this book says is possible; and to my dear original Editor Sheila Ableman, who nurtured all my BBC books to such successful birth and fruition; and to my cherished Editor, Joanne Osborn, who worked with me on many other successful publishing projects; to our superb artist and Mind Mapper, Alan Burton, the mnemonic memorability of whose artwork was matched only by the memorability of the witty and creative conversations about the artwork; and to my delightful BBC Editorial team, with a special thanks to Sally Potter and Kelly Davis.

# Foreword

by Dominic O'Brien, GMM

(FIRST AND 8 TIMES
WORLD MEMORY CHAMPION)

If I told you a story about a schoolboy who failed a number of his 'O' levels, left school aged sixteen, was told by his teachers that he would never amount to anything, but who eventually became the World Memory Champion, you would probably think I was a writer of fiction and that the story could not possibly be true. However, it *is* true. That 'failure of a lad' was me!

After leaving school, travelling and working at various jobs, I saw one day on television a man called Creighton Carvello memorise a pack of cards in just under three minutes. To me this was miraculous, although it was obviously not a trick. Creighton really had memorised the cards in that staggeringly short time.

I thought: 'I have a brain the same as he has. If he can do that marvellous feat, there must be a method by which I can also do it.' I set about training myself.

After a few months, I reached the 'Holy Grail' of three minutes. Wondering what to do next with my rapidly growing 'memory muscle', I heard of the first World Memory Championships in 1991, organised by the author of the book you are now reading, Tony Buzan. I entered the competition and after some mighty mental combat was declared the first World Memory Champion.

The foundation principles I used to achieve my World Championships are those you will find outlined in Tony Buzan's book. If you apply these principles to the matrices of knowledge that *Master Your Memory* so vividly portrays, you will be able to bestride both the world of memory and the world of knowledge simultaneously, giving yourself the advantages that I found such training and application gave to me: greater self-confidence, a growing mastery of my imagination, improved creativity, vastly improved perceptual skills, and, yes, a much higher IQ!

I feel honoured to be able to recommend this enlightening book, whose author has so many credentials. Besides holding the World Record for Creative IQ, Tony is the author of over eighty-five best sellers about the brain and learning. He has established the Brain Foundation, is co-founder of the Mind Sports Olympiad and creator of the now world-famous Mind Maps. He was named by Forbes Magazine as one of five top international lecturers, along with Mikhail Gorbachev, Henry Kissinger and Margaret Thatcher. To my mind, Tony is one of the world's most effective communicators, both verbally and in the written word.

Congratulations on starting a journey I know will change your life magnificently.

**Dominic O'Brien**

# Foreword

by *Dr Susan Whiting*, GMM

## (FIRST CONTESTED AND REIGNING WOMEN'S WORLD MEMORY CHAMPION)

All those who are seriously interested in improving their memories and that should mean everyone because we all have memories that can be improved – should study *Master Your Memory*.

I first came across this book some years ago, after I had given up a challenging professional career to look after my young family. Like many people in similar situations, I found myself needing some additional mental stimulation. Also, I suppose I had always been curious about memory techniques, especially when it came to learning more easily for exams and generally remembering all those things that life demands.

Fortunately, I was introduced to some of Tony Buzan's work and read a first edition of *Master Your Memory*. The book took me completely by surprise – I had no idea memorising information could be fun! After all, revising for exams was always tedious and, dare I say it, boring. Suddenly memorising became not only possible but pleasurable, and expanding my memory developed into a hobby.

Using the memory techniques that I found in Tony's work led on to other things, but it was certainly not a case of memorising for the sake of it. Having memorised many of the composers, I now understand and can relate better to the period in which they composed. My mind is somehow more focused and I appreciate their music even more. Because I now have a 'hook' for each of them in my brain, I can easily add further information.

Art and artists had never been part of my previous studies, but settling down and learning about them paid real dividends. For a start, it was enjoyable to learn something completely new to me, and when I visited the National Gallery you can imagine my delight when in room after room I discovered paintings I had memorised. I could tell my children all sorts of details about the artist and particular styles – a very satisfying experience, and not just because the children looked on Mummy with a new respect.

All of this culminated in my becoming the Women's World Memory Champion in 1994 and the first-ever female Grand Master of Memory in 1996.

How I wish that I had discovered these memory techniques earlier in life, before I had to take all my exams! You, the reader, have precisely that opportunity. This book will teach you how to learn in the most enjoyable way – but be warned, it can become quite addictive!

**Susan Whiting**

## Note on Recommended SEM³ locations

The Mnemons, a group found by the author and led by Dr Sue Whiting GMM, recommend and are using the following SEM3 locations for some of the major areas of knowledge:

| Polymathic Area | SEM³ Section |
|---|---|
| Geniuses | 1000–1199 |
| Artists | 1200–1399 |
| Composers | 1400–1599 |
| Scientists | 1600–1799 |
| Writers | 1800–1999 |
| Monarchs | 2000–2099 |
| Geography | 4000–4099 |
| Languages | 5000–5999 |
| Shakespeare | 7000–7499 |
| The Elements | 8000–8199 |
| The Human Body | 8200–8599 |
| Your Life | 9000–10,000+! |

# A Story You
# Will Remember for
# the Rest of Your Life

A student sat, frightened and enthralled. It was the first lesson of his first day at university. He, like the others in his class, had been forewarned that Professor Clark was not only the most brilliant graduate in English the university had ever had; he also looked down on his students from the height of his genius, and used his mental might to embarrass and confuse them. The Professor had deliberately come in late – to add to the tension!

Professor Clark strode nonchalantly into the room, and scanned the class with fiery eyes and a derisive smile.

Rather than going to his desk and ordering his papers in preparation, he stopped in *front* of his desk, clasped his hands firmly behind his back, and, with that same intent stare accompanied by a sneer, he said, *'First year English? I'll call the roll.'* He then began to bark out, machine-gun fashion, the names of the petrified students:

| | |
|---|---|
| 'Abrahamson?' | 'Here, sir!' |
| 'Adams?' | 'Here, sir!' |
| 'Barlow?' | 'Here, sir!' |
| 'Bush?' | 'Here, sir!' |
| 'Buzan?' | 'Here, sir!' . . . |

When he came to the next name he barked out 'Cartland', to which there was a deathly silence. Looking even more intently, the Professor, like some Grand Inquisitor, made soul-burning eye contact with each petrified student, as if expecting them to 'own up' to their already-identified name. Still receiving no response, he sighed deeply, and said, at twice the speed of normal speech: 'Cartland?... Jeremy Cartland, address 2761 West Third Avenue; phone number 794 6231; date of birth September 25th 1941;

mother's name Jean, father's name Gordon;... *Cartland!?'* Still no response! The silence became almost unbearable until, at exactly the right moment, he punctuated it with a shouted and terminal **'Absent!'**

And so on and on the Professor continued, calling the roll without hesitation. Whenever a student was absent he would go through the same 'Cartland Routine', presenting the entire database about the absentee even though he could have had no way of knowing, on this first day, who was going to be present and who was going to be absent, even though he had never seen any one of the students before. To everyone in the class it became increasingly apparent that he knew, in the same astounding detail, the same basic biographical information about each of them.

When he had completed the roll call with 'Zygotski?' ... 'Here, Sir!', he looked at the students sardonically and said, with a droll smile, 'That means Cartland, Chapman, Harkstone, Hughes, Luxmore, Mears and Tovey are absent!' He paused again, and then said: 'I'll make a note of that ... *some time!'*

So saying, he turned and left the room in stunned silence.

To the enthralled student it was one of those moments where a life's 'Impossible Dream' became possible: the dream of training his memory so that it could, in a multitude of special situations, function perfectly.

To be able to remember the names and dates of birth and death and all the important facts about the major artists, composers, writers and other 'greats'!

To be able to remember languages!

To be able to remember the giant catalogues of data from biology and chemistry!

To be able to remember any list he wanted!

To be able to remember like the Professor!

He leapt out of his seat, charged out of the classroom and caught up with Professor Clark in the hallway. He blurted out his question: 'Sir, how did you do *that?!'* With the same imperious manner, the Professor responded, 'Because, son, I'm a Genius!' And once again turned away, not hearing the student's mumbled response, 'Yes, sir, I know, but *still*, how did you *do* that?!'

For two months he pestered 'The Genius', who finally befriended him, and surreptitiously in class translated for him 'the magic formula' for constructing the memory system that had allowed him to so dazzle the students on that memorable first day.

For the next 20 years the student devoured every book he could find on memory, creativity and the nature of the human brain, with the vision constantly in mind of creating new Super Memory Systems that went beyond even what his Professor had been able to accomplish.

The first of these was the Memory Mind Map, a 'Swiss army knife thinking tool for the brain', that allowed the user not only to remember with accuracy and flexibility but also to create, plan, think, learn and communicate on the basis of that memory.

After the Mind Map came the giant, enjoyable and easy-to-use Super Matrix Memory System that would act as a database, allowing people to have immediate access to whatever major information structures were important and necessary to them.

After 25 years, the New System emerged. The enthralled student was me! The one to whom I offer this New System, with delight, is you.

# Master Your Memory
## and How to Use It

**2**

To start you off on what will be the major intellectual adventure of your life, the first section of this book gives you immediate proof that your own memory can easily and successfully complete a memory task normally only accomplished by one person in a hundred.

When you have proved that your own memory can work at this level, you will be shown how Memory (mnemonic) Systems were originally envisioned by the Ancient Greeks, and how they have been developed to the present day.

Next you will be introduced to the Memory Principles, which will give you the building blocks with which to structure your newly enhanced memory skills. This will be combined with a concomitant development of all your senses.

Following this, you will be introduced to the most up-to-date modern brain research, especially that involving the left and right cerebral cortex and the relationships between the upper, mid- and hind-brain. Here you will find out how the Memory Principles link with our modern knowledge of how your brain works.

Armed with the knowledge of how the Principles work, of how your senses can be enhanced, and of how your brain skills can be used appropriately, you will realise something amazing: that, in the process of successfully completing your first memory task, you not only used the fundamental principles invented by the Greeks, you also innocently applied state-of-the-art information on your brain to its excellent functioning!

From this you will be introduced to the first significant Memory System – the Major System. It is this system that has been used by most of the world's top memory performers, mnemonists and mental athletes such as those who compete in the Memoriad and the World Memory Championships. First you will be shown how to memorise a 10-item shopping list using the Major System, then immediately how to multiply your ability *10 times* in order to remember 100 items.

Taking the steps from 100 to 1000 to *10,000* may seem like an impossible dream. To show you that it is *completely* possible, you will be guided through recent experiments on learning and memory which prove that your brain can remember not only 10,000 items, but even more, with astonishing accuracy.

Further evidence will be drawn from some of the great brains in history (who had brains just like yours!), with examples showing the extraordinary memory feats of which the human brain is capable. I emphasise that their brains were the same as yours; they simply knew how to use them in the manner outlined in *Master Your Memory.*

By this stage you will be capable of absorbing comfortably the Self-Enhancing Master Memory Matrix ($SEM^3$). Having mastered the Matrix, you will be able to use it to learn and remember any significant database you wish.

You will then be in possession of the basic building blocks of knowledge in music, art, literature, science, astronomy, languages, history and world geography.

You will discover that, in the very act of developing your memory systems and of remembering the basic architectural structure of knowledge, you will be making your 'Memory Muscle' significantly more powerful and you will also be increasing your mental powers of concentration and creativity.

# Onword

We begin by proving to you that your memory is far better than you think!

# Proof That Your Memory Can Work: 3

## the Simple and Effective Link System

 **Preview**

- The Test
- Memorising the Planets of the Solar System

The memory test you are about to take involves the Planets of the Solar System. Having researched this area for the last 25 years, I have found that, in the average audience of 1000 people, the following statistics apply:

1   Nine hundred people out of 1000 have learnt and at some time memorised the Planets.
2   In each individual's lifetime, they have been 'exposed' to this information, either at school, or through various media, for a total number of hours ranging between 10 and 100.
3   One hundred out of 1000 *think* they know how many Planets there are in the Solar System.
4   Forty out of 1000 know they know how many.
5   Ten *think* they know the order of the Planets from the Sun to the farthest Planet.
6   Ten out of 1000 would be willing to bet on it!

The reason for this staggering loss of knowledge lies in the fact that we are never taught *how* to remember.

Check your knowledge and experience in this particular memory task:

- Did you learn the Planets of the Solar System, and if so, how many times and over what period of time?

- Do you know the currently accepted *number* of Planets in the Solar System?
- Do your know their *names*?
- Do you know the *normal order* of the Planets in the Solar System?

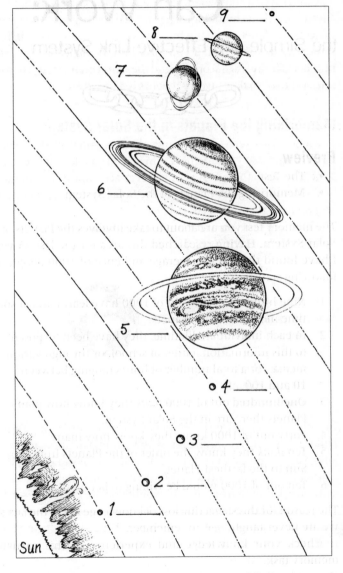

*Fig. 1* The nine Planets of our Solar System – one of the most difficult memory tasks confronted by the people on the third one! For how to memorise the Planets for the rest of your life, see page 20

## The Test

Write down the names of all the Planets of our Solar System. Now, using the illustration on page 19, with the Sun in the bottom left-hand corner, put the planet names where you think they should go next to the numbers 1–9. (Just to give you a clue – Sagittarius is not a planet!) When completed, see below for the correct planet order. Give yourself one mark for each planet correctly placed. If you have the correct planet name but in the wrong place, you score 0, in the same way as you would if you mixed up the digits of a telephone number! The average score around the world on this test is between one and two, so don't worry if yours is a low score.

## Memorising the Planets of the Solar System

The following exercise will change the way you use your memory for ever, increase your memory power, and enable you to complete a memory task that most people never accomplish in a lifetime!

Follow the instructions carefully, let your imagination run free, and prepare to be amazed.

There are nine known Planets in the Solar System.

In order from the Sun, they are:

1 Mercury (small)
2 Venus (small)
3 Earth (small)
4 Mars (small)
5 Jupiter (big)
6 Saturn (big)
7 Uranus (big)
8 Neptune (big)
9 Pluto (small)

In order to memorise the Planets for *life* you are going to use a Linking System, in conjunction with your imagination, to create a linked and fantastic story. If you follow it carefully and completely, it will be harder for you to forget than to remember!

Imagine that in front of you, where you are currently reading, is a glorious **SUN**. See it clearly, feel its heat, and admire its orange/red glow. Imagine, next to the Sun, a little (it's a little Planet) thermometer, filled with that liquid metal that measures temperature: **MERCURY**.

Imagine that the Sun heats up, and eventually becomes so hot that it bursts the thermometer. You see all over the desk or floor, in front of you, tiny balls of that liquid metal Mercury. Next you imagine that, rushing in to see what happens, and standing by your side, comes the most beautiful little goddess. Colour her, clothe her (optional!), perfume her, design her as you will. What shall we call our little goddess? Yes, **VENUS**!

You focus so intently on Venus with all your senses, that she becomes almost a living physical reality in front of you. You see Venus play like a child with the scattered mercury, and finally manage to pick up one of the mercury globules. She is so delighted that she throws it in a giant arc way up in the sky (which you see, as light glistens off it throughout its journey), until it hurtles down from on high and lands in your garden with a gigantic 'thump'!, which you both hear and feel as a bodily vibration.

And on what planet is your garden? **EARTH**.

Because of the power of her throw, and the height of the arc, when the globule lands it creates a small crater which sprays earth (EARTH) into your neighbour's garden.

In this fantasy you imagine that your neighbour is a little (it's a little Planet), red-faced (it's a red Planet), angry and war-like character carrying a chocolate bar in his leading hand! And who is this God of War? **MARS**.

Mars is furious that the earth has gone into his garden, and is just about to attack you when, striding on to the scene, comes a giant so large and powerful that he shakes the very foundations (and you must *feel them*) of where you are. See him standing a hundred feet tall, and make him as real as you made Venus. He tells Mars to calm down, which Mars immediately does, for this new giant, with a giant cow-lick 'J' on his forehead, is your best friend as well as being the king of the gods, the fifth Planet: **JUPITER**.

As you look up to the hundred-foot-high Jupiter, you see the word 'SUN' emblazoned in flashing gold letters across the giant T-shirt on his enormous chest. Each of these gigantic letters stands for the first letter of each of the next three big Planets of the Solar System: **SATURN, URANUS, NEPTUNE**.

Sitting on Jupiter's head, barking his little heart out with humour because he thinks the episode has been so hilarious, is a little (little because the Planet is so small) Walt Disney dog by the name of **PLUTO**.

Re-run this fantasy in your mind, and then see how difficult it is to forget!

In the continuing studies of people's memorisation of the Planets, it was found that, before memorising them with the Memory Principles:

(a)   Eight hundred out of 1000 people didn't really care about
the Planets and seldom paid attention to information
about them.
(b)   One hundred out of 1000 felt interested in the Planets.
(c)   One hundred out of 1000 were actively uninterested
and/or disliked the Planets.

After memorising the Planets with imagination and the Link
System, virtually every one of the 1000 became actively interested.

This on-going study illustrates the very significant fact that if the
human brain receives data that is rapidly forgotten or it becomes
confused, it will reject further data in that subject area. As time
goes on, the more information is presented to the brain in the given
area, the more it will block that information and the less it will
learn, often eventually blocking the information altogether.

If the brain, on the other hand, has information in an organised
and memorable matrix, each new bit of information will
automatically link to the existing information, naturally building
into the patterns of recognition, understanding and memory that
we call knowledge.

For example, if you hear that a space probe has been sent to
Venus and you do *not* know where Venus lies within the Solar
System, the first thing your brain will be confronted with is
confusion. You will not know which way the probe has gone
from the Earth, whether Venus is hot or cold, what its
relationship is to the Sun and why anyone should send a space
probe there in the first place. Consequently, you will react by
rejecting the information.

If, on the other hand, you *know* that Venus is the second Planet
out from the Sun, and is the one inside Earth's orbit that is nearest
to Earth, you will know that, as the space probe goes to Venus, it
will be going to a Planet that is nearer to the Sun and therefore
hotter than Earth. Your mind will therefore have a mental image
of direction, temperature, and nearness to Earth, and will *auto-matically* make appropriate associations. At the same time as your
mind is doing this, it will also be confirming your knowledge of
the other Planets. Thus, the more you know, *and remember*, the
more easily and automatically you begin to know more.

Thus you quickly come to realise that the more structured
knowledge you have in your memory, especially if it is in matrix
form, the easier it is to remember more. Your memory is so
extraordinary that, once given these basic matrices, it will continue
to link new information to them *without your conscious effort*. You

might wish to give yourself a head start by learning details of all the Planets (see chapter 19).

Conversely, if you do not have basic memory and knowledge structures, the more your mind confronts knowledge, the more it disconnects from it, leaving you with a growing 'memory of all that you have forgotten and not learnt'!

Thus, if you use your memory well, you can look forward to a life of increasing memory skills, expanding knowledge, accelerating ease of learning and, as a consequence of all these, greater mastery of your memory and therefore greater fun.

You have just completed a 'thought experiment' which used techniques identical to those used by the Great Geniuses throughout history. As soon as you phone or meet a friend or family member, teach them what you have just learnt – it will be an excellent review for you, will 'stamp' the memory more firmly in your brain, and will give them a useful gift. Encourage them to do the same, and within a few years you will have initiated that which will enable everybody on Earth to know where Earth is!

## Onword

In the next chapter you will be introduced to the history of memory (mnemonic) systems, and will receive the first of a number of insights into why your brain was able to do so remarkably well in the task you have just successfully completed.

# Memory –
## the Principles
### and Techniques

# 4

Did you know that over 95 per cent of people who drive a car have accomplished one of the most phenomenal forgetting tasks imaginable?!

They have driven their car to a shopping centre, an airport, a theatre, a friend's, and, having completed their tasks, have returned only to find they have *completely* lost (i.e. forgotten the location of) their car.

How is this *possible*?! It is a vehicle weighing three tonnes, it is theirs, they got into it, they drove it, they aimed it at the parking spot, they parked it, they shut off the engine, they got out of the car, they closed the door, and they locked it.

Surely the brain could not possibly forget such a thing?

As you read this chapter, you will realise that, not only were they capable of forgetting in such a situation, it is actually *predictable* that they would forget, for they did not apply the very essences of which memory is composed. Read on, and you will begin to see why . . .

# The Background

Before modern brain science had revealed, neurophysiologically and psychologically, the extraordinary power and potential of the human brain, the Greeks had discovered that mental performance could be enhanced enormously if certain techniques were used.

The Greeks developed fundamental memory systems called mnemonics, a name derived from their worship of the Goddess of Memory, Mnemosyne.

These mnemonic techniques were exchanged between members of the intellectual élite of the time, and were used to perform prodigious feats of memory in public that gained the performers personal, economic, political and military power.

The Greeks were thus '**Gladiators of the Mind**', their stadiums being intellectual amphitheatres, and their prime weapon Memory. They would hurl questions at each other concerning the number, names and order of the Greek City States, and the exact phrasing of quotes from their great literature and points of law.

Those who won would become the Senators, the heroes and the social leaders.

The techniques were based on fundamental principles that were, while being both easy and enjoyable to apply, profound in their effect on memory improvement.

# The Three Memory Principles

The Greeks discovered, by introspection, discussion and exchange, that memory was in major part based on **ASSOCIATION**; that it worked by linking things together. For example, as soon as your brain registers the word 'apple' it will remember (link) the colours, tastes, textures and smells of that fruit, as well as the experiences, friends and occasions connected with it.

In addition to Association, the Greeks realised that, for something to be remembered, it had to be a wonderful and multi-sensory **IMAGE**.

The third Pillar of Memory was **LOCATION**. In other words, for your brain to remember something that it has imagined and associated, it must also have that memory/image in a special location.

A library serves as a good analogy here. If you walked into a library that had a million books, and wished to find a specific one, would it be easier if all the books were piled up in the middle of the floor and you had to randomly search, or if all the books were beautifully and elegantly catalogued and ordered? Obviously the latter. *Master Your Memory* will help you do exactly the same for your brain!

## The 12 Memory Techniques

There are 12 special techniques which assist your memory in using association, image and location. If you take the first letter of each of the 12 key techniques, you will find they spell the phrase 'SMASHIN' SCOPE'. This is appropriate, because applying the 12 techniques does give a 'smashin' scope' to the vista of your memory.

### 1 ● Synaesthesia/Sensuality

Synaesthesia refers to the blending of the senses. Most of the great 'natural' memorisers, and all of the great mnemonists, developed an increased sensitivity in each of their senses, and then blended these senses to produce enhanced recall. In developing memory it was found to be essential to sensitise increasingly and train regularly your:

a) vision
b) hearing
c) smell
d) taste
e) touch
f) kinaesthesia – your awareness of bodily position and movement in space.

### 2 ● Movement

In any mnemonic image, movement adds another giant range of possibilities for your brain to 'link in' and thus remember. As your images move, make them three-dimensional.

### 3 ● Association

Whatever you wish to memorise, make sure you associate or link it to something stable in your mental environment.

### 4 ● Sexuality

We all have a good memory in this area. Use it!

### 5 ● Humour

The more ridiculous, absurd, funny and surreal you make your images, the more outstandingly memorable they will be. Have fun with your memory.

### 6 ● Imagination

Einstein said, 'Imagination is more important than knowledge. For knowledge is limited, whereas imagination embraces the entire world, stimulating progress, giving birth to evolution.' The more you apply your imagination to memory, the better your memory will be.

### 7 ● Number

Numbering adds specificity and efficiency to the principle of order and sequence.

### 8 ● Symbolism

Substituting a more meaningful image for an ordinary or boring image increases the probability of recall.

### 9 ● Colour

Where appropriate, and whenever possible, use the full range of the rainbow, to make your ideas more 'colourful' and therefore more memorable.

### 10 ● Order and/or Sequence

In combination with the other principles, order and/or sequence allows for much more immediate reference, and increases the brain's possibilities for 'random access'.

### 11 ● Positive images

In most instances, positive and pleasant images are better for memory purposes, because they make the brain want to return to the images. Certain negative images, even though they apply all the above principles, and though they are, in and of themselves, 'memorable', may be blocked by the brain because it finds the prospect of returning to such images unpleasant.

### 12 ● Exaggeration

In all your images, exaggerate size, shape, colour and sound.

Now that you have the three major principles and the 12 techniques, review perfectly in your imagination the Planets Story. As you go through it, step by step, check how many of the three principles the story is using, and how many of the 12 techniques.

Now you can understand why you did so brilliantly, and why, if you use your memory the way it was designed to be used, it will work wonders for you.

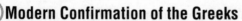

## Modern Confirmation of the Greeks

Recent brain research, especially in the area of the left and right cerebral cortex, has confirmed that all of us have, distributed throughout the most evolutionarily advanced part of our brains, an enormous range of mental skills that simply require appropriate training and development for them to manifest and grow. These 'left and right cortical skills' include the following:

1   Words
2   Order
3   Sequence
4   Number
5   Lists
6   Linearity
7   Analytical ability
8   Rhythm
9   Colour
10   Imagination
11   Re-creation
12   Dimension
13   Spatial awareness
14   *Gestalt* (whole picture)

In the hind- and mid-brain, and distributed in part throughout the upper brain, exist our additional mental abilities to:

1   See
2   Hear
3   Smell
4   Taste
5   Touch
6   Move in three-dimensional space
7   Respond
8   Emote

A quick check confirms the extraordinary similarity between what the Greeks discovered by self-analysis and practice, and what modern Science has discovered through the elegant rigours of the Scientific Method.

Armed with this double confirmation, it is possible to apply the Memory Principles with greater confidence and greater efficiency, guaranteeing hitherto undreamt-of improvements in your memory and general mental performance.

Now check the Planet Story once more, running through it very carefully, *this* time checking to see how many of the left and right cortical skills are employed in the system. You will find it is virtually all of them!

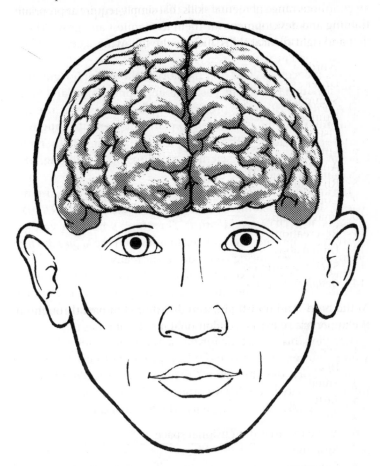

*Fig 2* The left and right hemispheres of the brain. Using the skill sets of *both* sides dramatically improves the memory.

## Creativity and Memory

From the theory you have understood and the exercise you have already completed on the memorisation of the Planets, the incredibly close link between memory *properly practised* and creativity will be starting to become clear.

The prime engine of your creativity is your IMAGINATION. The creative genius goes on imaginative journeys, taking people into original and previously unexplored realms. There, new ASSO-CIATIONS give rise to the new realisations that the world calls the creative breakthroughs – the works of mental genius that can shift the course of history.

So it was with Leonardo da Vinci, Darwin, Archimedes, Newton, Cézanne and Einstein.

Thus it becomes clear that memory is the use of imagination and association to hold the past in its appropriate place and to re-CREATE the past in the present; whereas creativity is the use of imagination and association to plant the present thought in the future, and to re-CREATE the present thought, whether it be a poem, a symphony, a scientific relationship, a building, or a spaceship, in some future time.

The important point here is that, although the name and purposes may be slightly different, the *underlying principles* of IMAGINATION and ASSOCIATION are identical. Therefore, whenever you are practising or applying memory techniques, you are *at the same time* practising and enhancing your powers of creativity.

These exercises are very much to the brain as gymnastic exercises are to the body. The more you exercise in the 'Gymnasium of Mnemonics', the more the 'muscles' of your memory and creativity will be developed.

Carrying this idea a little further, a new formula for developing your genius emerges: the more Energy you put into developing your Memory, the more your Creativity will grow. You have an infinite capacity to do this. In other words energy plus and 'into' memory equals infinite creativity. The formula can be written:

$$\textbf{E} \rightarrow \textbf{M} = \textbf{C}^{\infty}$$

The New Mental formula that demonstrates that if you put energy into your memory you will not only produce a perfect memory, but an expanding and potentially infinite creativity.

The SEM$^3$ Memory System allows you to embark on the journey towards both infinite memory and creativity.

## Memory Systems Are Not 'Tricks'

Because they are so incredibly effective, and because in recent centuries we have tended to denigrate the brain's abilities, many people think that memory systems must in some way be 'unreal' or 'not natural' and therefore some form of trick. However, our new knowledge of the function of the brain and memory has shown us that the reverse is true: that our 'normal' way of using our memories is unnatural and counter-productive, and that the initial realisations of early civilisations, such as the Greeks, were indeed the appropriate and *natural* first steps towards unlocking the limitless powers and vaults of our memories.

**Brain Bites**

In the last eight World Memory Championships, all the Grandmasters of Memory (and especially the World Memory Champions Dominic O'Brien and Dr Susan Whiting) have confirmed that the more they have practised with mnemonics, the more their natural and normal memories have expanded.

## Increasingly Advanced Systems

From the basic Link System, the early practitioners of memory realised that far more advanced and sophisticated systems could be developed (for further Special Systems, see *Use Your Memory* by the author, BBC Worldwide), and that the memorisation of much more complicated data could be made as easy as the memorisation of the Planets.

## Onword

One of the most successful of all such systems was the Major System, which is outlined in the next chapter. The Major System is the first giant step in mastering SEM$^3$.

# The Major System 5

 **Preview**
- Memorising the Major System Code
- Memorising Dates, Phone, Card and Code Numbers
- The Major System 'One Hundred'
- Making the Major System Your Own
- From 100 to 10,000 in One Easy Bound!

The secret code you are about to learn is the one that Professor Clark

surreptitiously put on the board on that magical day some 38 years ago

(see page 14).

You can now begin to see how Professor Clark performed his extraordinary memory feat in front of those entranced first-year university students. In order to remember all that specific information, he had to apply the Memory Principle of order and sequence. How did he do that? The Major System!

The Major System was devised in the mid-seventeenth century by Stanislaus Mink von Wennsshein. Von Wennsshein's objective was to create a memory system that would convert numbers into letters and letters into numbers, thus allowing the memoriser to make words out of any combination of numbers, and numbers out of any combination of letters.

In the eighteenth century the system was modified and improved by an Englishman, Dr Richard Grey.

In converting numbers to letters, the Major System has a special code, devised so that, by its very nature, it allows itself to be memorised. The code is as follows:

---

### SPECIAL CODE

| Numbers | | Associated Letters |
|---|---|---|
| 0 | = | s, z, soft c |
| 1 | = | d, t, th |
| 2 | = | n |
| 3 | = | m |
| 4 | = | r |
| 5 | = | l |
| 6 | = | j, sh, soft ch, dg, soft g |
| 7 | = | k, hard g, hard c, hard ch, ng, qu |
| 8 | = | f, v |
| 9 | = | b, p |

The vowels a, e, i, o, u and the letters h, w and y do not have numbers associated with them and are used simply as 'blanks' or fillers in the Key Memory Image Words you will soon be creating.

---

The numbers have been assigned these particular letters because they are especially memorable, as the following boxed explanation will reveal. The reason for the 'blank' letters is to enable you to make 'memory location' words easily.

The Major System's special code can be memorised almost instantaneously by applying the Memory Principles and Techniques you have already learnt, in the following way:

 ## Memorising the Major System Code

---

0   The letter *s*, or *z*, is the first sound of the word *zero*; *o* is the last letter.
1   The letters *d* and *t* have one downstroke.
2   The letter *n* has two downstrokes.
3   The letter *m* has three downstrokes.
4   The letter *r* is the last letter in the word *four*.
5   The letter *l* can be thought of as either the Roman numeral for 50 or a hand with five spread fingers, the index finger and thumb forming an L shape.
6   The letter *j* is the mirror image of 6.
7   The letter *k*, when seen as a capital, contains three number 7s.
8   The letter *f*, when handwritten, has two loops, similar to the number 8.
9   The letters *b* and *p* are mirror images of 9.

Once you have grasped the Special Code, it is possible to translate *any* number into any word and *any* word into any number.

You do this by decoding the number into its appropriate letters. Once you have the letters in order, you use the vowels and the letters *h, w* and *y*, which do not have any number-equivalent, as 'fillers' to help you make meaningful words.

For example, by referring to the Table opposite you can see that the number 11 translates into the letters *d* and *d*, giving the word *dad*. Similarly the number 43 translates to the letters *r* and *m*, giving the word *ram*.

---

Using one of the vowel 'fillers' (and in devising the word it is always best to try *a* before *e, e* before *i*, etc. because doing it in this way will always enable you to 'get it back' more rapidly and efficiently should you 'lose' it), you discover the word 'ram', which immediately translates back to the number 43.

---

Similarly, the number 82 translates to the letters *f* and *n*. Again, using the vowel 'filler', you immediately have the word *fan*, which itself translates back to the number 82.

## Memorising Dates, Phone, Card and Code Numbers

Using the Major System, you can thus translate any number (including phone numbers) or any date into meaningful words or phrases that make those numbers or dates simple and easy to recall at your convenience (see *Use Your Memory*).

Of equal importance, and what is to be the main focus of the remainder of *Master Your Memory*, is the fact that the Major System allows the brain to generate 100 Key Memory Images, to which you can then link whatever 100 items you wish to memorise. And, from this new base of 100, to leap to 1000, 10,000 and infinity!

## The Major System 'One Hundred'

The Major System 'One Hundred' consists of the numbers 0 to 99, and the words next to them (which become your permanent Key Memory Image Words). You make them up by taking the letters that the numbers represent, and adding a vowel or two in between in order to make appropriate words that, when decoded, translate back to the number. When checking which vowels work, always try *a* first, then *e*, then *i*, then *o*, then *u* and then *h, w* and *y*. Why?

|    | 0 | 1 | 2 | 3 | 4 | 5 | 6 | 7 | 8 | 9 |
|---|---|---|---|---|---|---|---|---|---|---|
| 00 | saw | day | Noah | ma | Ra | law | jaw | key | fee | bay |
| 10 | daze | dad | dan | dam | dairy | dale | dash | deck | daffy | dab |
| 20 | NASA | net | nan | name | Nero | nail | niche | nag | navy | nab |
| 30 | mace | mat | man | ma'am | mare | mail | mash | mac | mafia | map |
| 40 | race | rat | rain | ram | ra-ra | rail | rage | rack | rafia | rap |
| 50 | lace | lad | lane | lamb | lair | lily | lash | lake | lava | lab |
| 60 | chase | chat | chain | chime | chair | cello | cha-cha | check | chaff | chap |
| 70 | case | cat | can | cameo | car | call | cage | cake | café | cab |
| 80 | face | fad | fan | fame | fair | fall | fish | fag | fife | fab |
| 90 | base | bat | ban | bam! | bar | ball | bash | back | beef | babe |

Because should you ever be under stress or for some reason not able to recall your Key Memory Image, it will make it much easier for you to get it back if you have an easy, alphabetically based system to assist you.

The Basic One Hundred are presented in matrix form to enable you to check instantaneously in groups of tens, and to observe the patterns that ripple through the entire system, making it even easier to memorise.

As you memorise the Basic One Hundred, make sure that you regularly refer back, in your mind's eye, to the Special Code, and that each word in your Basic One Hundred has an especially clear *image* that, in itself, incorporates as many of the Memory Principles and Techniques as possible.

If, after continual practice, you note that a particular word is causing you difficulty, and that a different word using the same key letters is constantly imaging itself in your mind, feel free to use the word which your own mind recalls more easily.

To assist you in memorising the rarer words in the Basic One Hundred: the word Ra (4) refers to the straw raft/boat that the explorer Thor Heyerdahl used to prove that earlier civilisations could have travelled the major oceans; Dab (19) is a flat fish like a sole; Nan (22) is a large, flat Indian bread; and Fife (88) is a small, shrill flute used with a drum in military music.

### The First Ten

In order to make this task easier for you, we are going to concentrate first on the numbers 1 to 10. We are then going to imagine that you have a shopping list of 10 items to recall, and that you have no pen or scrap of paper to write it down (which is often a waste of time anyway, as many people forget where they have put the piece of paper!).

You are then going to use mnemonic techniques, and most of the skills of your left and right cortex, to enable you to memorise your list perfectly in order, perfectly in reverse order, and perfectly at random!

Let us imagine you wish to remember the following shopping list:

| | | | |
|---|---|---|---|
| 1 | Bananas | 6 | Potatoes |
| 2 | Apples | 7 | Tomatoes |
| 3 | Shoe polish | 8 | Flour |
| 4 | Toothpaste | 9 | Bread |
| 5 | A mug | 10 | Oranges |

Using the Major System, and applying the Memory Principles and Techniques exactly as you did when memorising the Planets, you might memorise the shopping list in the following way:

1   **1 – Day/Bananas**: Instead of the dawn rising (a good image for day), imagine a giant banana oozing up above the horizon, suffusing the sky with a yellow light. As you did with number 1, see, smell, taste and touch the banana.

2   **2 – Noah/Apples**: In this example you might imagine Noah standing at the front of his ark in the middle of the storm, juggling with beautiful bright red and green apples, taking scrumptious bites out of them as he juggles, and throwing them one by one to all the animals on the ark, they too delighting in the feast!

3   **3 – Ma/Shoe polish**: Imagine your Ma or a friend's Ma polishing a pair of beautiful leather shoes. See the scene extremely clearly. Smell both the leather and the polish. Hear the moving brush across the leather. And then to add humour, imagine that your mother decides to polish her own face!

The more you invent your own exaggerated images the better, for personal association is virtually always more memorable than that suggested or given by someone else. With the remaining seven items, therefore, apply the Memory Principles to the shopping list, making sure that whenever you are in doubt, you add more imagination and more sensuality. Once you have applied the Memory Principles to the memorisation of the list, test yourself, or get someone else to test you. Should you miss an item, go back to it, analyse where the weakness was, and strengthen your association.

By the time you have finished the full 10, you will have advanced from the basic Link System that you used for memorising the Planets, to the first Great Peg System. Peg Systems, like the Major System, use special, permanent and standard lists of Key Memory Images, on which you can attach whatever you wish to memorise, as you have just done with the first 10.

To prove just how good you are, and without looking at either the Major System itself on page 35 or the shopping list on page 36, jot down the first 10 words of the Major System, and the shopping items you memorised with them.

## Making the Major System Your Own

For the next two to three days, play with the Major System, refining your Key Memory Images, accelerating your speed, and making sure that in the memorisation of it you use the Memory Principles and Techniques and all your cortical skills. This system should become as natural to you as your name, address and phone number. For advanced particular applications of this system, see *Use Your Memory*. The rest of *Master Your Memory* uses the Major System to help you leap from 100 to 10,000 Key Memory Images, and also to give you the ultimate 'Memory Gymnasium'.

## From 100 to 10,000 in One Easy Bound!

Having established the Basic One Hundred, it is now possible, using a system which helps memorise itself, to develop the 10,000 memory system: The Self-Enhancing Master Memory Matrix (SEM$^3$).

SEM$^3$ will enable you to memorise not only all the information contained in *Master Your Memory*, but *any* list that may be of importance to you. For those of you using the Universal Personal Organiser (UPO) diary system (available from the Buzan Organization, see page 192), SEM$^3$ will also enable you to memorise, should you wish, not only the major events of each year of your life but *every day* of your life!

# Onword

The following chapter proves that you can do it,
explains the Self-Enhancing Master Memory Matrix in detail,
and shows you how to use and apply it.

# The Self-Enhancing Master Memory Matrix (SEM³): the Total Learning Memory Technique

# 6

> Before developing a system for the memorisation of 10,000 items,
> it is important to find out whether the brain can easily handle such
> a matrix. Both research and history indicate that the human brain
> can handle it with ease.

## The Experimental Evidence

In 1970, Ralph N. Haber reported the following experiment in *Scientific American:* subjects were shown a series of 2560 photographic slides at a rate of one every ten seconds. The total of seven hours of viewing was split into several separate sessions over a period of days, and, one hour after the last slide had been shown on the last day, the subjects were tested for recognition. They were shown 280 pairs of slides in which one member of each pair was a picture from the series they had seen, while the other was from a similar set which they had not seen. On average their recognition, even after such a drawn-out showing, was between 85 to 95 per cent accurate.

A second experiment was performed in which the presentation rate was speeded up ten times, to one image every second, and the results were identical.

A third experiment, in which the new high rate of presentation was maintained, but the pictures were shown as a mirror image, still produced identically high results.

Haber commented: 'these experiments with pictorial stimulae suggest that *recognition of pictures is essentially perfect.* The results would probably have been the same if we had used 25,000 pictures instead of 2500.'

In a further experiment reported by R. S. Nickerson in the *Canadian Journal of Psychology*, subjects were presented, at the rate of one per second, with 600 pictures, and tested immediately after the presentation. Recognition accuracy was 98 per cent.

Nickerson expanded on this research, subsequently presenting subjects with 10,000 pictures, making sure that the pictures were vivid (i.e. applied the Mnemonic Principles). With the vivid pictures, subjects were recalling 9996 out of 10,000 correctly!! When these results were extrapolated, it was estimated by the experimenters that if the subjects had been shown a million pictures rather than 10,000, they would have recognised 986,300.

The conclusion was: 'the capacity of recognition memory for pictures is almost limitless, when measured under appropriate conditions', according to Lionel Standing in his article 'Learning 10,000 Pictures' in the *Quarterly Journal of Experimental Psychology.*

With this evidence, it becomes apparent that the Self-Enhancing Master Memory Matrix, if used in conjunction with the Memory Principles, can be easily handled by your brain. Further evidence from the great memorisers confirms this.

## The Great Memorisers

The great memorisers had brains which were the same as everyone else's. They simply used them more effectively. Pick your own favourites from those that follow, and make them your role models. This will be the first step in building up your internal intellectual master-mind group of teachers and guides.

1  **Antonio di Marco Magliabechi** was able to read entire books, and memorise them without missing a single word or punctuation mark. He eventually memorised the entire library of the Grand Duke of Tuscany.

2  **Professor A.C. Aitken**, Professor of Mathematics at the University of Edinburgh, was easily able to remember the first 1000 decimal places of the value of Pi – forwards and backwards.

3   The American, **Daniel McCartney**, in the nineteenth
century, could tell, at the age of 54, what he had been
doing on every day since early childhood. He could give the
exact date, and weather conditions during the day, and say
what he had eaten for breakfast, lunch and supper on any
given day.

4   **Christian Friedrich Heinecken** at the age of 10 months
was able to speak and repeat every word said to him. By the
age of three he had memorised most of world history and
geography, and had similarly memorised Latin and French.

5   **Paul Charles Morphy** was a chess champion who could
remember every move of every game that he had played
throughout his championship career, including those he had
played while blindfolded. His claims were backed up by the
fact that nearly 400 of his games were preserved only because
he was able to dictate them *long* after the event, and have the
moves confirmed by his opponents and the judges present.

6   **Themistocles** was able to remember the 20,000 names of
the citizens of Athens.

7   **Xerxes** was reputed to be able to recall the names of the
100,000 men in his armies.

8   **Cardinal Messofanti**, a nineteenth-century linguist, was
able to memorise the vocabulary of between 70 and 80
languages, including Latin, Greek, Arabic, Spanish, French,
German, Swedish, Portuguese, English, Dutch, Danish,
Russian, Polish, Bohemian, Serbian, Hungarian, Turkish,
Irish, Welsh, Albanian, Sanskrit, Persian, Georgian, Armen-
ian, Hebrew, Chinese, Coptic, Ethiopian and Amharic.

9   **The Shass Pollak** Jews of Poland were able to remember
the exact position on the page of every word in each of the
12 volumes of the *Talmud*.

10   **Lengthy religious books**, such as the *Talmud* and the even
larger *Vedic Scriptures* of ancient India, were also passed
down by memory.

11   **Dr Susan Whiting**, Women's World Memory Champion,
has memorised well over 5000 bits of data using $SEM^3$ (see
page 10).

12   **Dominic O'Brien**, six times World Memory Champion,
holds innumerable world records in memory, including a
pack of cards memorised in 33.8 seconds; 18 packs of cards
perfectly memorised in one hour; and over 2000 binary
digits memorised in less than 30 minutes!

| Thousands | | 0–991 | 100–199 | 200–299 | 300–399 | 400–499 | 500–599 | 600–699 | 700–799 | 800–899 | 900–999 |
|---|---|---|---|---|---|---|---|---|---|---|---|
| 100–999 | Vision | – | Dinosaur | Nobility | Moonlight | Ravine | Lightning | Church | Concorde | Fire | Painting |
| 1000–1999 | Sound | Sing | Drum | Neigh | Moan | Roar | Lap | Shh | Gong | Violin | Piano |
| 2000–2999 | Smell | Seaweed | Tar | Nutmeg | Mint | Rose | Leather | Cheese | Coffee | forest | Bread |
| 3000–3999 | Taste | Spaghetti | Tomato | Nuts | Mango | Rhubarb | Lemon | Cherry | Custard | Fudge | Banana |
| 4000–4999 | Touch | Sand | Damp | Newspaper | Mud | Rock | Lather | Jelly | Grass | Velvet | Bark |
| 5000–5999 | Sensation | Swimming | Dancing | Nuzzling | Mingling | Rubbing | loving | Shaking | Climbing | Flying | Peace |
| 6000–6999 | Animals | Zebra | Dog | Newt | Monkey | Rhinocerous | Elephant | Giraffe | Kangaroo | Fox | Bear |
| 7000–7999 | Birds | Seagull | Duck | Nightingale | Magpie | Robin | Lark | Chicken | Kingfisher | Flamingo | Peacock |
| 8000–8999 | Rainbow | Red | Orange | Yellow | Green | Blue | Indigo | Violet | Black | Grey | White |
| 9000–9999 | Solar-system | Sun | Mercury | Venus | Earth | Mars | Jupiter | Saturn | Uranus | Neptune | Pluto |

# The Self-Enhancing Master Memory Matrix (SEM$^3$)

The Self-Enhancing Master Memory Matrix allows you, by using the same Memory Principles, to expand from 100 to 10,000 as quickly as you can visualise.

Using the Basic One Hundred from the Major System, you multiply this system by 10, giving you a system of 1000; you then multiply the 1000 system by 10, giving you a system of 10,000.

To create the list of 1000 (0–999), you use the Basic One Hundred, repeated in different aspects of your visual senses.

To create the system of 10,000, you once again use the Basic One Hundred in multiple ways, incorporating each of your senses of vision, sound, smell, taste, touch and sensation, as well as basic data from the physical kingdoms.

By creating a system using such elements, you are at the same time using all of those aspects of your brain that feed your memory skills. You are creating a giant mental gymnasium, which will allow you not only to memorise any list you wish, but which will at the same time provide you with on-going mental work-outs that increase every aspect of your 'Mental Muscle' while simultaneously giving you the opportunity to play infinite games. You construct your Self-Enhancing Master Memory Matrix in the following manner:

| | |
|---|---|
| 100–999 | Vision |
| 1000–1999 | Sound |
| 2000–2999 | Smell |
| 3000–3999 | Taste |
| 4000–4999 | Touch |
| 5000–5999 | Sensation |
| 6000–6999 | Animals |
| 7000–7999 | Birds |
| 8000–8999 | The Rainbow |
| 9000–9999 | The Solar System |

For the numbers 100 to 999 you use **VISION**; in other words, you focus on you *seeing* the image you wish to remember as your Key Memory Image. For 1000 to 1999, you use **SOUND**, focusing on your *hearing* for each image. For 2000 to 2999, you use your sense of **SMELL**, focusing on your memory images of this sense. And so on, for each thousand, using, sequentially, **TASTE**, **TOUCH**, **SENSATION**, **ANIMALS**, **BIRDS**, **THE COLOURS OF THE RAINBOW** and **THE SOLAR SYSTEM**.

For each separate 100 of each 1000, you have a specific Vision, a specific Sound, a specific Smell, etc. Thus, referring to the Matrix on page 42, your specific visions for the separate 100s from 100 to 999 are Dinosaur, Nobility, Moonlight, Ravine, Lightning, Church, Concorde, Fire and Painting.

For example, keeping 0–99 as your Basic 100 Matrix, and using nine Vision-images to get you from 100 to 999, you would do the following:

101 might simply be a giant dinosaur with its head rising above the horizon next to the sun at the beginning of a new *day;* 140 would be your same dinosaur leading an incredibly noisy, thundering and exciting dinosaur *race.* Whatever you wish to memorise as your 101st or 140th items would be attached to these SEM$^3$ images using the Basic Memory Principles.

Moving up in the first 1000, all still related to the first of your synaesthesia elements, Vision, all items from 700 to 799 would still be the basic code items, but in this instance connected to the image of Concorde. Thus 706 might be Concorde with its bent nose as a giant jaw; 795 could be Concorde with a giant ball for its wheels. Again, any item you wish to attach to these images would be attached using the Memory Principles.

Similarly, for 3000 to 3999, each separate hundred in the progression would have a Taste image attached to the basic hundred, in this instance Spaghetti, Tomato, Nuts, Mango, Rhubarb, Lemon, Cherry, Custard, Fudge and Banana.

To enable you to identify and memorise SEM$^3$ more easily, a matrix of the 100 divisions is on page 42.

To gain access to any number from 0 to 9999, you use the simple mental process outlined in the section entitled How to Use Your Self-Enhancing Master Memory Matrix (page 46).

When creating your images, which you should do as a game, as well as a mental exercise and mental brain training, make sure that in your Key Memory Images for each of the different senses, you emphasise the sense. Thus, for 4143, touch combined with damp combined with ram, but your main memory device here is to *feel* the wetness of its fur, its horns, its muzzle, and the smell of damp fur.

By using this Self-Enhancing Master Memory Matrix, you will not only be developing a system that enables you to memorise 10,000 items with the ease of Haber and Nickerson's experimental subjects, but you will also be training each one of your sensory areas, which will have a profound and positive influence on all other aspects of your life. This will include a positive influence on your health. Inability to remember, and subsequent frustration and annoyance at that inability, is often a major cause of stress and disease. This in itself creates a worsening memory. By using SEM$^3$, you will be reversing the trend.

In many ways you will be creating a positive spiral in which the more you practise your Memory Techniques, the more your general memory will improve; the more you add your knowledge lists to your memory matrix, the more you will be increasing the probability of automatic learning; and the more you do all this, the more automatically *all* of your various intelligences and mental skills will be improved.

The following chapters outline many of the major memory lists which, like the Planets, are supposed to be learnt for life but which are usually forgotten. Once they are learnt, they form giant foundations from which your brain can, with the ease and facility of 'The Greats', continue on its journey to wisdom.

The Superlist chapters are as follows:

 8 Artists
 9 Composers
10 Writers
11 Geniuses
12 Shakespeare
13 Vocabulary
14 Languages
15 Countries/Capitals
16 Kings and Queens of England
17 Human Body – Musculature
18 Elements
19 Solar System
20 Memorising Your Life

The suggested approach to the following Superlists, is to select the ones you wish to memorise, organise your Self-Enhancing Master Memory Matrix appropriately, and commence the exercise of remembering them. Throughout, apply the Memory Principles and Techniques.

To assist you with the construction and organisation of your Superlists refer to the Note on page 11 for recommended SEM$^3$ locations. From this point on, it is useful to develop further

*How to Use Your Self-Enhancing Master Memory Matrix*

## MAJOR SYSTEM – BASIC 100

To find the number 46

1) Go DOWN tens column on left to 40
2) Go ALONG 0–9 line to right till under 6

NOTE: all 40 numbers begin with R
    6 is *sh* or soft *ch*
    The word for 46 is RaGE

| TENS | 0 | 1 | 2 | 3 | 4 | 5 | 6 | 7 | 8 | 9 |
|---|---|---|---|---|---|---|---|---|---|---|
| 0–9 | | | | | | | | | | |
| 10–19 | | | | | | | | | | |
| 20–21 | | | | | | | | | | |
| 30–39 | | | | ↑ | | | | | | |
| 40–49 | ↑ | | | | | | →X | | | |
| 50–59 | | | | | | | | | | |
| 60–69 | | | | | | | | | | |
| 70–79 | | | | | | | | | | |
| 80–89 | | | | | | | | | | |
| 90–99 | | | | | | | | | | |

Another example
Find the word for 85
1) DOWN tens column to 80
2) ALONG 0–9 line to 5

NOTE:  Letter for 8 is F
        Letter for 5 is L

1st vowel that 'fits' is 'a'
The word is FaLL

## SEM³ 100-9999

To find the number 6374

1) Go DOWN thousands column on left to 6000
2) Go ALONG 0–9 hundreds line 300–399
3) REFER to BASIC 100 MATRIX
    DOWN tens column to 70
    ALONG 0–9 line to 4

| THOUSANDS | 0–99 | 100's | 200's | 300's | 400's | 500's | 600's | 700's | 800's | 900's |
|---|---|---|---|---|---|---|---|---|---|---|
| 100–999 | | | | → | | | | | | |
| 1000–1999 | | | | | | | | | | |
| 2000–2999 | | | | | | | | | | |
| 3000–3999 | | | | → | | | | | | |
| 4000–4999 | | | | | | | | | | |
| 5000–5999 | | | | | | | | | | |
| 6000–6999 | ↑ | ↑ | ↑ | X | | | | | | |
| 7000–7999 | | | | | | | | | | |
| 8000–8999 | | | | | | | | | | |
| 9000–9999 | | | | | | | | | | |

So 6000 – ANIMALS: 300 – MONKEY: 74 – CAR
Your memory hooks could be 'an enormous monkey squeezing into a tiny open sports car'!
For 2351?
2000 – SMELL: 300 – MINT: 51– LAD
A powerfully minty smelling lad!
or 5800 – a flying saw!

*For application and rules see pages 34 –8*

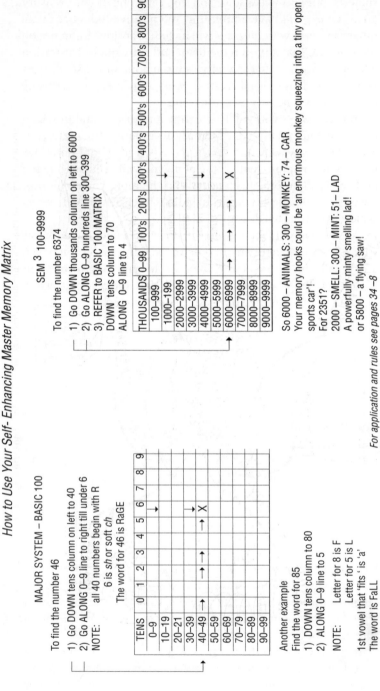

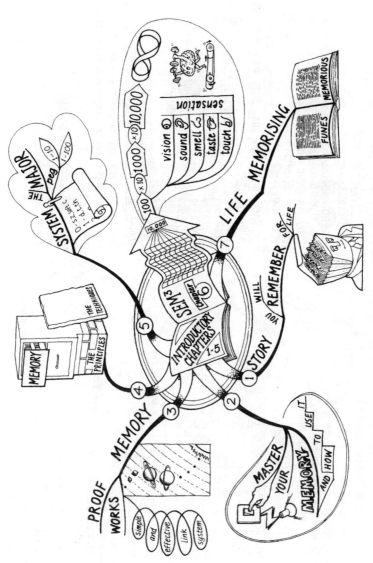

*Fig 3* Mind Map of chapters 1–6. When you make your own Mind Maps, you can use colour to make the various branches even more memorable.

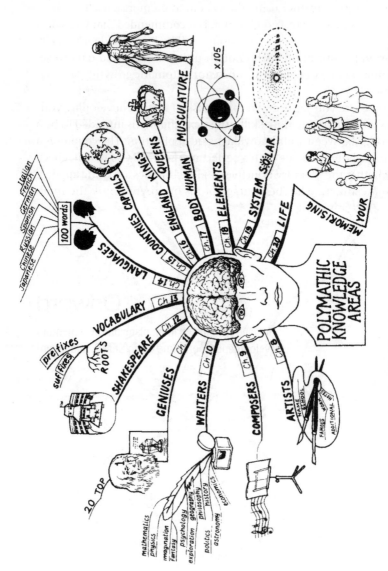

*Fig 4* Mind Map of chapters 8–19, the Polymathic Knowledge areas. To make *Master Your Memory* even *more* memorable, why not colour each branch of the Mind Map as you complete each chapter?

memory matrices for any other lists that would be useful to you, and to make a habit of memorising at least one new list per year.

Should you wish to remember the matrix itself, the Basic One Hundred can be used to memorise each of the Key Words in the matrix, thus further using the system to memorise itself.

To get you off to a good start, it is recommended that you select from *Master Your Memory* at least two of the lists included. This will provide your brain with enough units of organised data to set your 'memory engine' on course for automatic growth! (*See Note, page 11.*)

Before you settle down to the task of further developing your extraordinary memory skills, the next chapter is intended to be a bridge between your knowledge and application. The chapter is a story about someone with a perfect memory. As you read it, check whether the Memory Principles and Techniques are being applied, and estimate what percentage of his brain you think the main character is using!

## Onword

After you have read the chapter, plan your own memory development programme using SEM $^3$, and begin!

# Memorising a Life:
## the Story of Funes,
## the Memorious

# 7

Critics are still trying to determine whether the following story
by Jorge Luis Borges was a fabrication, a brilliant work of imagination,
or true reportage. In view of what you have read so far, decide for yourself.

Is it possible? Did Funes really exist? Is the story true?

## Funes, the Memorious

I remember him (I scarcely have the right to use this ghostly verb;
only one man on earth deserved the right, and he is dead), I remember
him with a dark passionflower in his hand, looking at it as no one has
ever looked at such a flower, though they might look from the twilight
of day until the twilight of night, for a whole life long. I remember
him, his face immobile and Indian-like, and singularly *remote*, behind
his cigarette. I remember (I believe) the strong delicate fingers of the
plainsman who can braid leather. I remember, near those hands, a
vessel in which to make maté tea, bearing the arms of the Banda
Oriental;* I remember, in the window of the house, a yellow rush mat,
and beyond, a vague marshy landscape. I remember clearly his voice,
the deliberate, resentful nasal voice of the old Eastern Shore man,
without the Italianate syllables of today, I did not see him more than
three times; the last time, in 1887. . .

That all those who knew him should write something about him
seems to me a very felicitous idea; my testimony may perhaps be

*The Eastern Shore (of the Uruguay River); now the Orient Republic of Uruguay.
– Editor's note.

the briefest and without doubt the poorest, and it will not be the least impartial. The deplorable fact of my being an Argentinian will hinder me from falling into a dithyramb – an obligatory form in the Uruguay, when the theme is an Uruguayan.

*Littérateur, slicker, Buenos Airean*: Funes did not use these insulting phrases, but I am sufficiently aware that for him I represented these unfortunate categories. Pedro Leandlo Ipuche has written that Funes was a precursor of the superman, 'an untamed and vernacular Zarathustra'; I do not doubt it, but one must not forget, either, that he was a countryman from the town of Fray Bentos, with certain incurable limitations.

My first recollection of Funes is quite clear, I see him at dusk, some time in March or February of the year '84. That year, my father had taken me to spend the summer at Fray Bentos. I was on my way back from the farm in San Francisco with my cousin Bernardo Haedo. We came back singing, on horseback; and this last fact was not the only reason for my joy. After a sultry day, an enormous slate-grey storm had obscured the sky. It was driven on by a wind from the south; the trees were already tossing like madmen; and I had the apprehension (the secret hope) that the elemental downpour would catch us out in the open. We were running a kind of race with the tempest. We rode into a narrow lane which wound down between two enormously high brick footpaths. It had grown black of a sudden; I now heard rapid almost secret steps above; I raised my eyes and saw a boy running along the narrow, cracked path as if he were running along a narrow, broken wall. I remember the loose trousers, tight at the bottom, the hemp sandals; I remember the cigarette in the hard visage, standing out against the by now limitless darkness. Bernardo unexpectedly yelled to him: 'What's the time, Ireneo?' Without looking up, without stopping, Ireneo replied: 'In ten minutes it will be eight o'clock, child Bernardo Juan Francisco'. The voice was sharp, mocking.

I am so absentminded that the dialogue which I have just cited would not have penetrated my attention if it had not been repeated by my cousin, who was stimulated, I think, by a certain local pride and by a desire to show himself indifferent to the other's three-sided reply.

He told me that the boy above us in the pass was a certain Ireneo Funes, renowned for a number of eccentricities, such as that of having nothing to do with people and of always knowing the time, like a watch. He added that Ireneo was the son of Maria Clementine Funes, an ironing woman in the town, and that his father, some people said, was an 'Englishman' named O'Connor, a doctor in the salting fields, though some said the father was a horse-breaker, or scout, from the province of El Salto. Ireneo lived with his mother, at the edge of the country house of the Laurels.

In the years '85 and '86 we spent the summer in the city of Montevideo. We returned to Fray Bentos in '87. As was natural, I inquired after all my acquaintances, and finally, about 'the chronometer Funes'. I was told that he had been thrown by a wild horse at the San Francisco ranch, and that he had been hopelessly crippled. I remember the impression of uneasy magic which the news provoked in me: the only time I had seen him we were on horseback, coming from San Francisco, and he was in a high place; from the lips of my cousin Bernardo the affair sounded like a dream elaborated with elements out of the past. They told me that Ireneo did not move now from his cot, but remained with his eyes fixed on the backyard fig tree, or on a cobweb. At sunset he allowed himself to be brought to the window. He carried pride to the extreme of pretending that the blow which had befallen him was a good thing .
. . Twice I saw him behind the iron gate which sternly delineated his eternal imprisonment: unmoving, once, his eyes closed; unmoving also, another time, absorbed in the contemplation of a sweet-smelling sprig of lavender cotton.

At the time I had begun, not without some ostentation, the methodical study of Latin. My valise contained the *De viris illustribus* of Lhomond, the *Thesaurus* of Quicherat, *Caesar's Commentaries,* and an odd-numbered volume of the *Historia Naturalis* of Pliny, which exceeded (and still exceeds) my modest talents as a Latinist. Everything is noised around in a small town; Ireneo, at his small farm on the outskirts, was not long in learning of the arrival of these anomalous books. He sent me a flowery, ceremonious letter, in which he recalled our encounter, unfortunately brief, 'on the seventh day of February of the year '84,' and alluded to the glorious services which Don Gregorio Haedo, my uncle, dead the same year, 'had rendered to the Two Fatherlands in the glorious campaign of Ituzaingó,' and he solicited the loan of any one of the volumes, to be accompanied by a dictionary 'for the better intelligence of the original text, for I do not know Latin as yet.' He promised to return them in good condition, almost immediately. The letter was perfect, very nicely constructed; the orthography was of the type sponsored by Andres Bello: *i* for *y, j* for *g.* At first I naturally suspected a jest. My cousins assured me it was not so, that these were the ways of Ireneo. I did not know whether to attribute to impudence, ignorance, or stupidity, the idea that the difficult Latin required no other instrument than a dictionary; in order fully to undeceive him I sent the *Gradus ad Parnassum* of Quicherat, and the Pliny.

On 14 February, I received a telegram from Buenos Aires telling me to return immediately, for my father was 'in no way well'. God forgive me, but the prestige of being the recipient of an urgent telegram, the desire to point out to all of Fray Bentos the contradiction between the negative form of the news and the positive adverb, the temptation to dramatise my sorrow as I feigned a virile stoicism, all no doubt distracted me from the possibility of anguish. As I packed my valise, I noticed that I was missing the *Gradus* and the volume of the *Historia Naturalis.* The *Saturn* was to weigh anchor on the morning of the next day; that night, after supper, I made my way to the house of Funes. Outside, I was surprised to find the night no less oppressive than the day.

Ireneo's mother received me at the modest ranch.

She told me that Ireneo was in the back room and that I should not be disturbed to find him in the dark, for he knew how to pass the dead hours without lighting the candle. I crossed the cobblestone patio, the small corridor; I came to the second patio. A great vine covered everything, so that the darkness seemed complete. Of a sudden I heard the high-pitched, mocking voice of Ireneo. The voice spoke in Latin; the voice (which came out of the obscurity) was reading, with obvious delight, a treatise or prayer or incantation. The Roman syllables resounded in the earthen patio; my suspicion made them seem undecipherable, interminable; afterwards, in the enormous dialogue of that night, I learned that they made up the first paragraph of the twenty-fourth chapter of the seventh book of the *Historia Naturalis.* The subject of this chapter is memory; the last words are *ut nihil non iisdem verbis redderetur auditum.*

Without the least change in his voice, Ireneo bade me come in. He was lying on the cot, smoking. It seems to me that I did not see his face until dawn; I seem to recall the momentary glow of the cigarette. The room smelled vaguely of dampness. I sat down, and repeated the story of the telegram and my father's illness.

I come now to the most difficult point in my narrative. For the entire story has no other point (the reader might as well know it by now) than this dialogue of almost a half-century ago. I shall not attempt to reproduce his words, now irrecoverable. I prefer truthfully to make a résumé of the many things Ireneo told me. The indirect style is remote and weak; I know that I sacrifice the effectiveness of my narrative; but let my readers imagine the nebulous sentences which clouded that night.

Ireneo began by enumerating, in Latin and Spanish, the cases of prodigious memory cited in the *Historia Naturalis:* Cyrus, king of the Persians, who could call every soldier in his armies by name; Mithridates Eupator, who administered justice in the twenty-two languages of his empire; Simoniedes, inventor of mnemotechny; Metrodorus, who practised the art of repeating faithfully what he heard once. With evident good faith Funes marvelled that such things should be considered marvellous. He told me that previous to the rainy afternoon when the blue-tinted horse threw him, he had been – like any Christian – blind, deaf-mute, somnambulistic, memoryless. (I tried to remind him of his precise perception of time, his memory for proper names; he paid no attention to me.) For nineteen years, he said, he had lived like a person in a dream: he looked without seeing, heard without hearing, forgot everything – almost everything. On falling from the horse, he lost consciousness; when he recovered it, the present was almost intolerable it was so rich and bright; the same was true of the most ancient and most trivial memories. A little later he realised that he was crippled. This fact scarcely interested him. He reasoned (or felt) that immobility was a minimum price to pay. And now, his perception and his memory were infallible.

We, in a glance, perceive three wine glasses on the table; Funes saw all the shoots, clusters, and grapes of the vine. He remembered the shapes of the clouds in the south at dawn on the 30th of April of 1882, and he could compare them in his recollection with the marbled grain in the design of a leatherbound book which he had seen only once, and with the lines in the spray which an oar raised in the Rio Negro on the eve of the battle of the Quebracho. These recollections were not simple; each visual image was linked to muscular sensations, thermal sensations, etc. He could reconstruct all his dreams, all his fancies. Two or three times he had reconstructed an entire day. He told me: *I have* more *memories in myself alone than all men have had since the world was a world.* And again: *My dreams are like your vigils.* And again, toward dawn: *My memory, sir, is like a garbage disposal.*

A circumference on a blackboard, a rectangular triangle, a rhomb, are forms which we can fully intuit; the same held true with Ireneo for the tempestuous mane of a stallion, a herd of cattle in a pass, the ever-changing flame or the innumerable ash, the many faces of a dead man during the course of a protracted wake. He could perceive I do not know how many stars in the sky.

These things he told me; neither then nor at any time later did they seem doubtful. In those days neither the cinema nor the phonograph yet existed; nevertheless, it seems strange, almost incredible, that no one should have experimented on Funes. The truth is that we all live by leaving behind; no doubt we all profoundly know that we are immortal and that sooner or later every man will do all things and know everything.

The voice of Funes, out of the darkness, continued. He told me that toward 1886 he had devised a new system of enumeration and that in a very few days he had gone beyond twenty-four thousand. He had not written it down, for what he once mediated would not be erased. The first stimulus to his work, I believe, had been his discontent with the fact that 'thirty-three Uruguayans' required two symbols and three words, rather than a single word and a single symbol. Later he applied his extravagant principle to the other numbers. In place of seven thousand thirteen, he would say (for example) *Máximo Perez;* in place of seven thousand fourteen, *The Train;* other numbers were *Luis Melián Lafinur, Olimar, Brimstone, Clubs, The Whale, Gas, The Cauldron, Napoleon, Agustín de Vedia.* In lieu of five hundred, he would say *nine.* Each word had a particular sign, a species of mark; the last were very complicated . . . I attempted to explain that this rhapsody of unconnected terms was precisely the contrary of a system of enumeration. I said that to say three hundred and sixty-five was to say three hundreds, six tens, five units: an analysis which does not exist in such numbers as *The Negro Tmoteo* or *The Flesh Blanket.* Funes did not understand me, or did not wish to understand me.

Locke, in the seventeenth century, postulated (and rejected) an impossible idiom in which each individual object, each stone, each bird and branch had an individual name; Funes had once projected an analogous idiom, but he had renounced it as being too general, too ambiguous. In effect, Funes not only remembered every leaf on every tree of every wood, but even every one of the times he had perceived or imagined it. He determined to reduce all of his past experience to some seventy thousand recollections, which he would later define numerically. Two considerations dissuaded him: the thought that the task was interminable and the thought that it was useless. He knew that at the hour of his death he would scarcely have finished classifying even all the memories of his childhood.

The two projects I have indicated (an infinite vocabulary for the natural series of numbers, and a usable mental catalogue of all the images of memory) are lacking in sense, but they reveal a certain stammering greatness. They allow us to make out dimly, or to infer, the dizzying world of Funes. He was, let us not forget, almost incapable of general, platonic ideas. It was not only difficult for him to understand that the generic term *dog* embraced so many unlike specimens of differing sizes and different forms; he was disturbed by the fact that a dog at three-fourteen (seen in profile) should have the same name as the dog at three-fifteen (seen from the front). His own face in the mirror, his own hands, surprised him on every occasion. Swift writes that the emperor of Lilliput could discern the movement of the minute hand; Funes could continuously make out the tranquil advances of corruption, of caries, of fatigue. He noted the progress of death, of moisture. He was the solitary and lucid spectator of a multiform world which was instantaneously and almost intolerably exact. Babylon, London, and New York have overawed the imagination of men with their ferocious splendour; no one, in those populous towers or upon those surging avenues, has felt the heat and pressure of a reality as indefatigable as that which day and night converged upon the unfortunate Ireneo in his humble South American farmhouse. It was very difficult for him to sleep. To sleep is to be abstracted from the world; Funes, on his back in his cot, in the shadows, imagined every crevice and every moulding of the various houses which surrounded him. (I repeat, the least important of his recollections was more minutely precise and more lively than our perception of a physical pleasure or a physical torment.) Toward the east, in a section which was not yet cut into blocks of homes, there were some new unknown houses. Funes imagined them black, compact, made of a single obscurity; he would turn his face in this direction in order to sleep. He would also imagine himself at the bottom of the river, being rocked and annihilated by the current.

Without effort, he had learned English, French, Portuguese, Latin. I suspect, nevertheless, that he was not very capable of thought. To think is to forget a difference, to generalise, to abstract. In the overly replete world of Funes there was nothing but details, almost contiguous details.

The equivocal clarity of dawn penetrated along the earthen patio.

Then it was that I saw the face of the voice which had spoken all through the night. Ireneo was nineteen years old; he had been born in 1868; he seemed as monumental as bronze, more ancient than

Egypt, anterior to the prophecies and the pyramids. It occurred to me that each one of my words (each one of my gestures) would live on in his implacable memory; I was benumbed by the fear of multiplying superfluous gestures.

Ireneo Funes died in 1889, of a pulmonary congestion.

1942                                    *Translated by* ANTHONY KERRIGAN
(Taken from *Fictions* by Jorge Luis Borges, published by
J. Calder, London.)

# The Artists 8

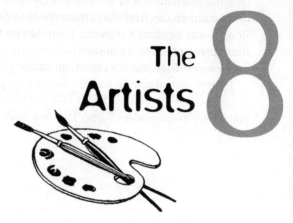

Leonardo da Vinci said, if you wish to develop an all round mind,
make sure you 'study the Science of Art, and study the Art of Science'.

The great artists have spearheaded mankind's research into
the nature of our perception. They have also recorded human
history with an elegance at least equal to that of the poets,
novelists, dramatists and literary historians. Knowing their names,
birthplaces, dates of birth and death, and some of their famous
works, places them, as you did with the Planets, in a context and
perspective that allows you automatically and continually to learn
more about them as you progress through life.

In memorising the great Artists, Composers and Writers, you
might, for example, choose SEM³ numbers from 1000 to 1300, if
you had already used your first thousand. Let's assume that Leonardo
da Vinci was your number 1020. Your SEM³ Key Memory Image is
the number 20 (NASA) joined with the Sound-image of Singing.

To remember that Leonardo was a high Renaissance (rebirth)
inventor, one of his famous works being 'Virgin of the Rocks', you
could imagine a beautiful dale in which he was sitting at an easel,
painting the scene perfectly on a giant canvas while singing an
operatic aria (to remind you that he was Italian). To remember
Renaissance (rebirth) you could place a little baby by Leonardo's
side helping him with his paints. At the end of the dale you could
imagine a giant outcrop of rocks on which a beautiful virgin was
trapped and calling for help (you might even make her a bit like
the Mona Lisa). To remember the dates 1452 to 1519, you would

take the numbers 4 = R, 5 = L, 2 = N; 5 = L, 1 = T or D, 9 = B, and make word images from them that related to da Vinci. For example, Renaissance Leading Naturalist; Leonardo Da Vinci's Burial. Apply these principles and examples to memorising whichever of the major knowledge matrices most appeals to you.

Information about each of the major European artists has been categorised under four headings to aid you both in speed of reference and ability to memorise: Name, Famous work and School.

## Onword

Every time you see an advertisement for an art exhibition in future, the images and information pertaining to that exhibition and artist will add to your growing body of Art Knowledge, and will increase your knowledge of this most important area to your continuing advantage.

1 **Duccio di Buoninsegna**   1255–1318   Italian
*Famous work:* Christ Entering Jerusalem
(Cathedral Museum, Siena)
*School:* Sienese, Pre-Renaissance

2 **Giotto**   1267–1337   Italian
*Famous work:* The Lamentation
(Fresco in Arena Chapel, Padua)
*School:* Florentine, Pre-Renaissance

3 **Simone Martini**   1284–1344   Italian
*Famous work:* The Annunciation (Uffizi Gallery, Florence)
*School:* Sienese

4 **Jan van Eyck**   1385/90–1441   Dutch
*Famous work:* Giovanni Arnolfini and his Bride
(National Gallery, London)
*School:* Flemish

5 **Fra Angelico**   1387–1455   Italian
*Famous work:* The Annunciation
(Monastery of San Marco, Florence)
*School:* Florentine

**6 Paolo Uccello**   1397–1475   Italian
*Famous work:* The Battle of San Romano
(National Gallery, London)
*School:* Florentine

**7 Roger van der Weyden**   1399–1464   Flemish
*Famous work:* The Deposition (Prado, Madrid)
*School:* Flemish

**8 Masaccio**   1401–1428   Italian
*Famous work:* The Rendering of the Tribute Money
(Brancacci Chapel, Santa Maria del Carmine, Florence)
*School:* Florentine

**9 Piero della Francesca**   1410/20–1492   Italian
*Famous work:* The Resurrection
(Palazzo Cominale, Boreo San Sepolcro)
*School:* Umbrian

**10 Giovanni Bellini**   1430–1516   Italian
*Famous work:* The Madonna of the Meadow
(National Gallery, London)
*School:* Venetian

**11 Andrea Mantegna**   1431–1506   Italian
*Famous work:* Christ Praying in the Garden
(National Gallery, London)
*School:* Mantuan

**12 Luca Signorelli**   1441/50–1523   Italian
*Famous work:* Pan as God of Music
(Staatliche Museen, Berlin)
*School:* Umbrian

**13 Sandro Botticelli**   1445–1510   Italian
*Famous work:* The Birth of Venus (Uffizi Gallery, Florence)
*School:* Florentine

**14 Hieronymus Bosch**   1450–1516   Dutch
*Famous work:* The Garden of Earthly Delights
(Prado, Madrid)
*School:* Flemish

**15 Leonardo da Vinci**   1452–1519   Italian
*Famous work:* The Virgin of the Rocks (Louvre, Paris)
*School:* Florentine

**16 Albrecht Dürer**   1471–1528   German
*Famous work:* The Four Apostles (Pinakothek, Munich)
*School:* German

**17 Michelangelo Buonarroti**   1475–1564   Italian
*Famous work:* Sistine Chapel Ceiling (Vatican, Rome)
*School:* Florentine

**18 Mathis Grünewald**   1470/80–1528   German
*Famous work:* The Crucifixion, from the Isenheim
Altarpiece (Musée Unterlinden, Colmar)
*School:* German

**19 Giorgione**   1477–1510   Italian
*Famous work:* Fête Champêtre (Louvre, Paris)
*School:* Venetian

**20 Raphael**   1483–1520   Italian
*Famous work:* The School of Athens (Vatican, Rome)
*School:* Florentine

**21 Titian**   1487–1576   Italian
*Famous work:* The Death of Acteon
(National Gallery, London)
*School:* Venetian

**22 Antonio Correggio**   1489/94–1534   Italian
*Famous work:* Danae (Galleria Borghese, Rome)
*School:* Parma

**23 Hans Holbein (The Younger)**   1497–1543   German
*Famous work:* Portrait of Erasmus (Louvre, Paris)
*School:* German

**24 Jacopo Tintoretto**   1518–1594   Italian
*Famous work:* The Last Supper (Santa Marciola, Venice)
*School:* Venetian Mannerist

**25 Pieter Bruegel (The Elder)**   1520/30–1569   Flemish
*Famous work:* The Parable of the Blind
(Museo Nazionale, Naples)
*School:* Flemish

**26 Paolo Veronese**   1528–1588   Italian
*Famous work:* Christ in the House of Levi (Academy, Venice)
*School:* Venetian

**27 El Greco**   1541–1614   Greek
*Famous work:* The Assumption of the Virgin
(1577, Art Institute of Chicago)
*School:* Spanish (by adoption)

**28 Annibale Carracci**   1560–1609   Italian
*Famous work:* Hercules at the Crossroads
*School:* Bolognese, Classical

**29 Michelangelo Merisi
da Caravaggio**   1571–1610   Italian
*Famous work:* The Supper at Emmaus
(National Gallery, London)
*School:* Independent Tenebrist

**30 Sir Peter Paul Rubens**   1577–1640   Flemish
*Famous work:* Descent from the Cross (Antwerp Cathedral)
*School:* Flemish, Baroque

**31 Frans Hals**   1581–1666   Dutch
*Famous work:* The Laughing Cavalier
*School:* Dutch

**32 Georges de la Tour**   1593–1652   French
*Famous work:* The Adoration of the Shepherds
(Louvre, Paris)
*School:* Lorraine

**33 Nicolas Poussin**   1595–1665   French
*Famous work:* Rape of the Sabine Women
(Metropolitan Museum, New York)
*School:* French, worked mainly in Rome, Classical

**34 Francisco de Zurbárán**   1598–1664   Spanish
*Famous work:* St Francis of Assisi (Lyon Museum)
*School:* Spanish

**35 Sir Anthony van Dyck**   1599–1641   Flemish
*Famous work:* Charles I of England (The King Hunting),
(Louvre, Paris)
*School:* Flemish

**36 Diego Rodriguez de Silva
y Velasquez**   1599–1660   Spanish
*Famous work:* Las Meninas (Prado, Madrid)
*School:* Spanish

**37  Gelle Claude (Claude Lorraine)**   1600–1682   French
*Famous work:* The Embarkation of the Queen of Sheba
(National Gallery, London)
*School:* French, Romantic Classicist

**38  Bartolome Esteban Murillo**   1617/18–1682   Spanish
*Famous work:* The Immaculate Conception
(Seville Museum)
*School:* Spanish

**39  Harmensz van Rijn Rembrandt**   1606–1669   Dutch
*Famous work:* The Night Watch (Rijksmuseum, Amsterdam)
*School:* Dutch

**40  Jacob van Ruisdael**   1628/29–1682   Dutch
*Famous work:* The Bleaching Ground
(National Gallery, London)
*School:* Dutch

**41  Jan Vermeer**   1632–1675   Dutch
*Famous work:* The Music Lesson (Queen's Gallery, London)
*School:* Dutch

**42  Jean Antoine Watteau**   1684–1721   French
*Famous work:* The Pilgrimage to the Island of Cythera
(Louvre, Paris)
*School:* French

**43  Giovanni Batista Tiepolo**   1696–1770   Italian
*Famous work:* Antony and Cleopatra Frescoes
(Palazzo Labia, Venice)
*School:* Venetian

**44  William Hogarth**   1697–1764   English
*Famous work:* Marriage à la Mode
(National Gallery, London)
*School:* English

**45  (Giovanni) Antonio Canaletto**   1697–1768   Italian
*Famous work:* The Basin of San Marco on Ascension Day
(National Gallery, London)
*School:* Venetian

**46  Jean Baptiste Simeon Chardin**   1699–1779   French
*Famous work:* Kitchen Still Life
(Museum of Fine Arts, Boston)
*School:* French

**47 François Boucher**    1703–1770   French
*Famous work:* The Triumph of Venus (Stockholm Museum)
*School:* French, Rococo

**48 Sir Joshua Reynolds**    1723–1792   English
*Famous work:* Mrs Siddons as the Tragic Muse
(Huntingdon Library, San Marino, California)
*School:* English

**49 George Stubbs**    1724–1806   English
*Famous work:* White Horse Frightened by a Lion
(Walker Art Gallery, Liverpool)
*School:* English

**50 Thomas Gainsborough**    1727–1788   English
*Famous work:* Mr and Mrs Andrews
(National Gallery, London)
*School:* English

**51 Jean Honoré Fragonard**    1732–1806   French
*Famous work:* The Pursuit (Frick Collection, New York)
*School:* French, Rococo

**52 Joseph Wright of Derby**    1734–1797   English
*Famous work:* Experiment on a Bird in an Air Pump
(Tate Gallery, London)
*School:* English

**53 Francisco de Goya y Lucientes**    1746–1828   Spanish
*Famous work:* The Third of May (Prado, Madrid)
*School:* Spanish

**54 Jacques Louis David**    1748–1825   French
*Famous work:* Death of Marat
(Royal Museum of Fine Art, Brussels)
*School:* French, Neo-classical

**55 William Blake**    1757–1827   English
*Famous work:* Dante Meeting Beatrice in Paradise
(Tate Gallery, London)
*School:* English

**56 Caspar David Friedrich**    1774–1840   German
*Famous work:* Man and Woman Gazing at the Moon
(National Galerie, Berlin)
*School:* German Romantic

**57  Joseph Mallord William Turner**   1775–1851   English
*Famous work:* Rain, Steam and Speed
(National Gallery, London)
*School:* English

**58  John Constable**   1776–1837   English
*Famous work:* The Haywain (National Gallery, London)
*School:* English

**59  Jean Auguste Dominique Ingres**   1780–1867   French
*Famous work:* Le Bain Turc (Louvre, Paris)
*School:* French, Neo-classical

**60  John Sell Cotman**   1782–1842   English
*Famous work:* Chirk Aqueduct (Victoria and Albert Museum)
*School:* English, Norwich

**61  Théodore Géricault**   1791–1824   French
*Famous work:* The Raft of the Medusa (Louvre, Paris)
*School:* French, Romantic

**62  Jean Baptiste Camille Corot**   1796–1875   French
*Famous work:* Souvenir de Morte Fontaine (Louvre, Paris)
*School:* French

**63  Eugene Delacroix**   1798–1863   French
*Famous work:* Liberty on the Barricades
*School:* French, Romantic

**64  Jean François Millet**   1814–1875   French
*Famous work:* The Angelus (Louvre, Paris)
*School:* French, Romantic

**65  Gustave Courbet**   1819–1877   French
*Famous work:* Good Morning, Monsieur Courbet
(Musee Fabre, Montpellier)
*School:* French, Realist

**66  William Holman Hunt**   1827–1910   English
*Famous work:* The Light of the World
(Keble College, Oxford)
*School:* English, Pre-Raphaelite Brotherhood

**67  Arnold Bocklin**   1827–1901   Swiss
*Famous work:* Island of the Dead
(Metropolitan Museum, New York)
*School:* Swiss, Romantic

**68 Camille Pissaro**     1831–1903    French
*Famous work:* The Red Roofs (Louvre, Paris)
*School:* French Impressionist (Landscape)

**69 Edouard Manet**     1832–1883    French
*Famous work:* A Bar at the Folies-Bergère
(Courtauld Institute, London)
*School:* French, Urban Impressionist

**70 Edgar Degas**     1834–1917    French
*Famous work:* The Dancing Class (Musée d'Orsay, Paris)
*School:* French, Urban Impressionist

**71 Paul Cézanne**     1839–1906    French
*Famous work:* Mont Sainte-Victoire (Museum of Art,
Philadelphia)
*School:* French, Post Impressionist

**72 Odilon Redon**     1840–1916    French
*Famous work:* Silence (Museum of Modern Art, New York)
*School:* French Symbolist

**73 Claude Monet**     1840–1926    French
*Famous work:* Water Lilies Series (Louvre, Paris)
*School:* French Impressionist

**74 Pierre-Auguste Renoir**     1841–1919    French
*Famous work:* Ball at the Moulin de la Galette
(Musée d'Orsay, Paris)
*School:* French Impressionist

**75 Paul Gauguin**     1848–1903    French
*Famous work:* Riders on the Beach
(Folkwang Museum, Essen)
*School:* French, Post Impressionist

**76 Vincent van Gogh**     1853–1890    Dutch
*Famous work:* Sunflowers (National Gallery, London)
*School:* French, Post Impressionist

**77 Georges Seurat**     1859–1891    French
*Famous work:* The Bathers at Asnières
(National Gallery, London)
*School:* French, Pointillist

**78  Walter Richard Sickert**    1860–1942   English
*Famous work:* The Eldorado, Paris
(University of Birmingham)
*School:* Camden Town Group (Post Impressionist)

**79  Edvard Munch**    1863–1944   Norwegian
*Famous work:* The Scream (National Gallery, Oslo)
*School:* Norwegian, Precursor of Expressionism

**80  Wassily Kandinsky**    1866–1944   Russian
*Famous work:* Improvisation No. 30 (Cannons)
(Art Institute of Chicago)
*School:* Der Blaue Reiter (The Blue Horseman), Abstract

**81  Pierre Bonnard**    1867–1947   French
*Famous work:* Coffee (Tate Gallery, London)
*School:* Intimist

**82  Henri Matisse**    1869–1954   French
*Famous work:* Red Studio
(Museum of Modern Art, New York)
*School:* Fauve

**83  Giacomo Balla**    1871–1958   Italian
*Famous work:* Dog on a Leash
(A. Congere Goodyear, New York)
*School:* Italian Futurist

**84  Georges Rouault**    1871–1958   French
*Famous work:* The Apprentice (Musée d'Art Moderne, Paris)
*School:* School of Paris, Independent Expressionist

**85  Piet Mondrian**    1872–1944   Dutch
*Famous work:* Broadway Boogie Woogie
(Museum of Modern Art, New York)
*School:* De Stijl, Neoplasticism, Abstract

**86  Paul Klee**    1879–1940   German/Swiss
*Famous work:* Landscape with Yellow Birds
(Doetsch-Benzinger Collection, Basel)
*School:* Associated with Der Blaue Reiter, Independent

**87  Fernand Léger**    1881–1955   French
*Famous work:* Les Fumeurs (Smokers)
(Guggenheim Museum, New York)
*School:* Cubist

**88  Pablo Ruiz y Picasso**    1881–1973    Spanish
*Famous work:* Guernica (Prado, Madrid)
*School:* Cubist

**89  Georges Braque**    1882–1963    French
*Famous work:* Studio IX (Maeght Collection, Paris)
*School:* Cubist

**90  Max Beckman**    1884–1950    German
*Famous work:* Departure
(Museum of Modern Art, New York)
*School:* Expressionist

**91  Percy Wyndham Lewis**    1884–1957    English
*Famous work:* Portrait of Edith Sitwell
(Tate Gallery, London)
*School:* Vorticist (English Branch of Cubism/Futurism)

**92  Robert Delaunay**    1885–1941    French
*Famous work:* Window on the City No. 4
(Guggenheim Museum, New York)
*School:* School of Paris, Orphist

**93  Juan Gris**    1887–1927    Spanish
*Famous work:* Still Life in Front of an Open Window
(Arenburg Collection, Philadelphia Museum of Art)
*School:* Cubist

**94  Marc Chagall**    1887–1985    Russian
*Famous work:* I and the Village
(Museum of Modern Art, New York)
*School:* School of Paris, Independent Fantasist

**95  Giorgio de Chirico**    1888–1978    Italian
*Famous work:* Enigma of Arrival (Private Collection, Paris)
*School:* Italian Metaphysical

**96  Paul Nash**    1889–1946    English
*Famous work:* Totesmeer (Tate Gallery, London)
*School:* English Surrealist

**97 Max Ernst**    1891–1976    German
*Famous work:* Swamp Angel
(Macpherson Collection, Rome)
*School:* Surrealist

**98 Stanley Spencer**     1891–1959   English
*Famous work:* The Murals at Burghclere Chapel
*School:* Independent, Religious

**99 René Magritte**     1898–1967   Belgian
*Famous work:* The False Mirror (Museum of Modern Art, New York)
*School:* Surrealist

**100 Salvador Dali**     1904–1989   Spanish
*Famous work:* The Persistence of Memory (Museo Nacional Centro de Arte Reina Sophia, Madrid)
*School:* Surrealist

# The Composers 9

As artists record the visual history of the human race, so the great composers record the aural/musical history. Sound, as the basis for one of your five senses, hearing, is automatically a major memory device. It is also one of the areas of mental skill that is essential for the development of the Master Memory skill of synaesthesia – the blending of the senses for the enhancement of each and the correlative increase in mental skills, especially creativity and memory.

Once you have organised and memorised, using SEM³, the following list of composers and the major information about them, you will have created a foundation of musical knowledge that will allow your brain *automatically* to build multiple associations around each composer and each composer's music, and rapidly to integrate those into a growing fabric of delightful and spirit-enhancing knowledge.

When you hear for example on BBC Radio 3, that Smetana was originally known for his astounding energy and enthusiasm, that his two children died at an early age, and that he lost his life to the most debilitating disease, causing the physical disintegration of his brain, and yet that he still composed and recorded in intricate detail the nature of his decline and the nature of its effect on his memory, you will listen to his music with greater understanding and compassion, and similarly will know more about the historical times in which he lived.

# Onword

By using SEM3 in this way, you will be exploring, with the great historical and current musical brains, the human race's search, through the medium of sound, for an increasing understanding of its own nature.

1 **Philippe de Vitry**     1291–1361   French
*Famous work:* Impudenter circumivi/ Virtutibus
*Style:* Secular and of the Ars Nova
*Era:* Middle Ages

2 **Guillaume de Machaut**     1300–1377   French
*Famous work:* Messe de Notre Dame
*Style:* Sacred and secular
*Notes:* Well-respected statesman, cleric and poet
*Era:* Middle Ages

3 **Francesco Landini**     1325–1397   Italian
*Famous work:* Ecco la primavera
*Style:* Secular
*Notes:* Blind from childhood
*Era:* Middle Ages

4 **John Dunstable**     1390–1453   English
*Famous work:* O Rosa Bella
*Style:* Sacred and secular
*Notes:* Well known for 'singability' of his music
*Era:* Middle Ages

5 **Gilles de Bins Binchois**     1400–1460   Franco-Flemish
*Famous work:* Filles à marier
*Style:* Sacred and secular
*Era:* Renaissance

6 **Guillaume Dufay**     1400–1474   Franco-Flemish
*Famous work:* Se la face ay pale
*Style:* Sacred and secular
*Era:* Renaissance

7 **Johannes Ockeghem**     1410–1497   Franco-Flemish
*Famous work:* Missa cuiusvi toni
*Style:* Sacred and secular
*Era:* Renaissance

**8 Josquin Desprez**      1440–1521    Franco-Flemish
*Famous work:* Ave Maria
*Style:* Sacred and secular
*Era:* Renaissance

**9 Heinrich Isaac**      1450–1517    Flemish
*Famous work:* Choralis constantinus
*Style:* Sacred and secular vocal music
*Era:* Renaissance

**10 Andrea Gabrieli**      1510–1586    Italian
*Famous work:* Magnificat for 3 choirs and orchestra
*Style:* Sacred and madrigals
*Notes:* Introduced technique 'Cori spezzati' (spaced choirs)
*Era:* Renaissance

**11 Giovanni Pierluigi da Palestrina**      1525–1594    Italian
*Famous work:* Missa Papae Marcelli
*Style:* Sacred and secular vocal music
*Era:* Renaissance

**12 Orlande de Lassus**      1532–1594    Franco-Flemish
*Famous work:* Alma redemptoris mater
*Style:* Sacred and secular vocal music
*Era:* Renaissance

**13 William Byrd**      1543–1623    English
*Famous work:* Sing Joyfully/Ave Verum Corpus
*Style:* Sacred and secular choral music, vocal chamber music, instrumental and keyboard music
*Notes:* Described as 'Father of British Music'
*Era:* Renaissance

**14 Giulio Caccini**      1545–1618    Italian
*Famous work:* Toccate d'Intavolature di Cimbale e Organo
*Style:* Le Nuove Musiche
*Era:* Baroque

**15 Tomás Luis de Victoria**      1548–1611    Spanish
*Famous work:* Mass Laetatus Sum
*Style:* Songs in new styles
*Era:* Renaissance

**16 Luca Marenzio**    1553–1599    Italian
*Famous work:* Dolorosi martir
*Style:* Secular vocal music and sacred vocal music
*Era:* Renaissance

**17 Giovanni Gabrieli**    1555–1612    Italian
*Famous work:* Canzon XIII
*Style:* Sacred vocal music, instrumental music and secular
vocal music
*Era:* Renaissance

**18 Thomas Morley**    1557–1602    English
*Famous work:* Now Is the Month of Maying
*Style:* Secular and sacred vocal music, instrumental music
*Notes:* Specialised in Ballett Madrigals (light form of madrigal)
*Era:* Renaissance

**19 Carlo Gesualdo**    1560–1613    Italian
*Famous work:* Deh, coprite il bel seno
*Style:* Secular and sacred vocal music
*Era:* Renaissance

**20 John Bull**    1562–1628    English
*Famous work:* Fantasia
*Style:* Keyboard composer
*Era:* Renaissance

**21 John Dowland**    1563–1626    English
*Famous work:* In darkness let mee dwell
*Style:* Secular vocal, instrumental music
*Era:* Renaissance

**22 Claudio Monteverdi**    1567–1643    Italian
*Famous works:* Madrigals of Love and War, Il ritorno d'Ulisse
in patria (The return of Ulysses to his country)
*Style:* Secular vocal, sacred vocal, madrigals, operas
*Era:* Renaissance/Baroque

**23 Thomas Weelkes**    1575–1623    English
*Famous work:* As Vesta was from Latmos Hill descending
*Style:* Madrigals, sacred vocal and instrumental
*Era:* Renaissance

**24 Orlando Gibbons**    1583–1625    English
*Famous works:* This is the Record of John, The Silver Swan
*Style:* Vocal, sacred choral, keyboard and instrumental
music
*Era:* Renaissance

**25 Girolamo Frescobaldi**    1583–1643    Italian
*Famous work:* Capriccio sopra la battaglia
*Style:* Vocal and keyboard music
*Notes:* Known as 'A giant among organists'
*Era:* Baroque

**26 Heinrich Schütz**    1585–1672    German
*Famous works:* St Matthew's Passion, Christmas Oratorio
*Style:* Secular and sacred vocal music
*Era:* Baroque

**27 Francesco Cavalli**    1602–1676    Italian
*Famous work:* Ercole Amante (Hercules the Lover)
*Style:* Secular vocal
*Era:* Baroque

**28 Giacomo Carissimi**    1605–1674    Italian
*Famous work:* The Representation of the Body and Soul
*Style:* Sacred musical dramas
*Era:* Baroque

**29 Jean-Baptiste Lully**    1632–1687    Italian
*Famous work:* L'amour médecin
*Style:* Sacred choral music, comedy ballet, operas, ballets
and dance music
*Era:* Baroque

**30 Dietrich Buxtehude**    1637–1707    Danish
*Famous work:* Oratorios, cantatas, organ music
*Style:* Invented 'musica recitativa'
*Notes:* Began idea of evening music, public concerts in
churches and known as great influence on Bach
*Era:* Baroque

**31 Arcangelo Corelli**    1653–1713    Italian
*Famous work:* Christmas Concerto
*Style:* Church sonatas
*Era:* Baroque

**32 Henry Purcell**     1659–1695     English
*Famous works:* My heart is inditing, Fantasia upon One Note
*Style:* Secular and sacred choral music, instrumental and
keyboard music
*Era:* Baroque

**33 Alessandro Scarlatti**     1660–1725     Italian
*Famous work:* Le Teodora augusta
*Style:* Sacred and secular, choral and vocal music, operas,
instrumental music
*Era:* Baroque

**34 François Couperin**     1668–1733     French
*Famous work:* Concerts Royaux
*Style:* Keyboard music especially harpsichord, chamber
music, sacred and secular vocal music
*Era:* Baroque

**35 Antonio Vivaldi**     1678–1741     Italian
*Famous work:* The Four Seasons
*Style:* Concertos, operas, sacred choral music and chamber
music
*Era:* Baroque

**36 Georg Philipp Telemann**     1681–1767     German
*Famous work:* Musique de table
*Style:* Progressive composer
*Era:* Baroque

**37 Jean-Philippe Rameau**     1683–1764     French
*Famous work:* Hippolyte et Aricie
*Style:* Operas, keyboard music, chamber music,
sacred choral music
*Era:* Baroque

**38 Johann Sebastian Bach**     1685–1750     German
*Famous work:* St John's Passion
*Style:* Sacred choral, secular vocal, orchestral chamber
music, keyboard music, organ music
*Era:* Baroque

**39 Domenico Scarlatti**     1685–1757     Italian
*Famous work:* Essercizi per Gravicembalo
*Style:* Keyboard, sacred choral, instrumental and operas
*Era:* Baroque

**40  George Frideric Handel**      1685–1759
German/English
*Famous work:* Water Music
*Style:* Operas, oratorios, sacred vocal, secular vocal,
orchestral, chamber and keyboard music
*Era:* Baroque

**41  Christoph Willibald Gluck**      1714–1787   German
*Famous works:* Don Juan, Orfeo ed Euridice
*Style:* Operas, ballet, songs, sacred vocal and chamber music
*Era:* Classical

**42  Carl Philip Emanuel Bach**      1714–1788   German
*Famous work:* Rondo in E Flat
*Style:* Keyboard, orchestral, chamber and choral music
*Era:* Classical

**43  Franz Joseph Haydn**      1732–1809   Austrian
*Famous work:* The London Symphony
*Style:* Symphonies, keyboard and chamber music, operas,
oratorios, choral music
*Era:* Classical

**44  Johann Christian Bach**      1735–1782   German
*Famous work:* Concerted Symphony in E flat
*Style:* Orchestral, chamber, organ, keyboard, operas and
sacred music
*Era:* Classical

**45  Luigi Boccherini**      1743–1805   Italian
*Famous work:* String Quintet in E major, Opus 13 No. 5
*Style:* Chamber music, symphonies and concertos, opera
and sacred music
*Era:* Classical

**46  Muzio Clementi**      1752–1832   Italian
*Famous work:* Minuetto pastorale in D
*Style:* Composed for piano
*Notes:* Known as 'Father of pianoforte'
*Era:* Classical

**47  Wolfgang Amadeus Mozart**      1756–1791   Austrian
*Famous work:* The Magic Flute, Don Giovanni
*Style:* Operas, symphonies, concertos, choral music,
chambermusic, piano music, vocal music
*Era:* Classical

**48 Ignace Pleyel**     1757–1831   Austrian
*Famous works:* Sinfonies Concertantes
*Style:* Symphonies, chamber music
*Era:* Classical

**49 Ludwig van Beethoven**     1770–1827   German
*Famous works:* Pastoral Symphony, Fidelio
*Style:* Symphonies, concertos, choral music, piano music,
string quartets, chamber music, songs, opera
*Notes:* Radically transformed all the musical forms with
which he worked
*Era:* Classical

**50 Carl Maria von Weber**     1786–1826   German
*Famous works:* The Freeshooter, Invitation to the Dance
*Style:* Operas, orchestral music, piano music,
incidental music
*Era:* Romantic

**51 Gioacchino Rossini**     1792–1868   Italian
*Famous works:* Barber of Seville, William Tell
*Style:* Operas, sacred choral music, secular and
chamber music
*Era:* Romantic

**52 Franz Schubert**     1797–1828   Austrian
*Famous works:* Beautiful Maid of the Mill, The Trout Quintet
*Style:* Songs, orchestral, chamber, piano and operas
*Notes:* Died when only 31 years old
*Era:* Romantic

**53 Vincenzo Bellini**     1801–1835   Italian
*Famous work:* I Puritani
*Style:* Vocal, opera, songs and instrumental music
*Era:* Romantic

**54 Hector Berlioz**     1803–1869   French
*Famous works:* Symphonie Fantastique, Romeo et Juliette
*Style:* Opera, orchestral symphonies, sacred choral music,
secular choral music, vocal music
*Era:* Romantic

**55  Felix Mendelssohn**      1809–1847   German
*Famous works:* A Midsummer Night's Dream, The Hebrides
*Style:* Orchestral music, symphonies, chamber music, piano music, sacred choral music
*Era:* Romantic

**56  Frédéric Chopin**      1810–1849   Polish
*Famous work:* The Etudes
*Style:* Piano music, orchestral music, chamber music
*Era:* Romantic

**57  Robert Schumann**      1810–1856   German
*Famous works:* A Woman's Love and Life, Scenes from Faust
*Style:* Song, piano music, orchestral, chamber, opera and choral music
*Era:* Romantic

**58  Franz Liszt**      1811–1886   Hungarian
*Famous works:* The Hungarian Rhapsodies, Faust Symphony
*Style:* Orchestral music, piano music, choral music
*Era:* Romantic

**59  Richard Wagner**      1813–1883   German
*Famous work:* The Flying Dutchman
*Style:* Operas, orchestral music, songs
*Era:* Romantic

**60  Giuseppe Verdi**      1813–1901      Italian
*Famous works:* Rigoletto, Requiem
*Style:* Operas, sacred choral, secular choral, chamber music
*Era:* Romantic

**61  Bedrich Smetana**      1824–1884   Czechoslovak
*Famous works:* The Bartered Bride, Vltava
*Style:* Symphonic poems, chamber music and opera
*Era:* Turn of 19th Century

**62  Anton Bruckner**      1824–1896   Austrian
*Famous work:* Te Deum
*Style:* Symphonies, choral music, chamber music
*Era:* Turn of 19th Century

**63  Alexander Borodin**      1833–1887   Russian
*Famous work:* Prince Igor
*Style:* Symphonies and operas
*Era:* Turn of 19th Century

**64 Johannes Brahms**    1833–1897   German
*Famous works:* Hungarian Dance, Tragic Overture, German
Requiem
*Style:* Orchestral, chamber music, piano music, choral
music, songs
*Era:* Romantic

**65 Modest Mussorgsky**    1839–1881   Russian
*Famous work:* Sunless
*Style:* Operas, orchestral, songs and piano music
*Era:* Turn of 19th Century

**66 Pyotr Ilyich Tchaikovsky**    1840–1893   Russian
*Famous works:* Sleeping Beauty, The Nutcracker
*Style:* Operas, ballets, choral music, symphonies,
chamber music
*Era:* Turn of 19th Century

**67 Antonin Dvorak**    1841–1904   Czechoslovak
*Famous works:* New World Symphony,
The American Quartet
*Style:* Orchestral music, symphonies, operas,
chamber music, choral music
*Era:* Turn of 19th Century

**68 Nikolay Rimsky-Korsakov**    1844–1908   Russian
*Famous work:* The Snow Maiden
*Style:* Operas, orchestral works
*Era:* Turn of 19th Century

**69 Leos Janacek**    1854–1928   Czechoslovak
*Famous work:* The Cunning Little Vixen
*Style:* Operas, choral, vocal, orchestral, chamber music
*Era:* Turn of 19th Century

**70 Edward Elgar**    1857–1934   English
*Famous works:* Pomp and Circumstance, Enigma Variations,
The Apostles
*Style:* Orchestral, choral, chamber, songs, piano, incidental
*Era:* Turn of 19th Century

**71 Giacomo Puccini**    1858–1924   Italian
*Famous works:* La Bohème, Madame Butterfly
*Style:* Operas, choral music
*Era:* Turn of 19th Century

**72 Hugo Wolf**     1860–1903   Austrian
*Famous work:* Der Corregidor
*Style:* Songs, opera, orchestral, chamber music
*Era:* Turn of 19th Century

**73 Gustav Mahler**     1860–1911   Austrian
*Famous works:* The Resurrection, Songs of the Wayfarer,
The Boy's Magic Horn
*Style:* Symphonies, songs, choral music
*Era:* Turn of 19th Century

**74 Claude Debussy**     1862–1918   French
*Famous works:* Prélude à l'Après-midi d'un Faune, La Mer
*Style:* Orchestral, ballet, piano, chamber music
*Era:* Turn of 19th Century

**75 Richard Strauss**     1864–1949   German
*Famous works:* The Cavalier of the Rose, A Woman without
a Shadow
*Style:* Orchestral, operas, choral music, songs
*Era:* Turn of 19th Century

**76 Jean Sibelius**     1865–1957   Finnish
*Famous works:* Tone Poem en Saga, Night Ride and Sunrise,
The Tempest
*Style:* Orchestral, incidental, choral, chamber
*Era:* Turn of 19th Century

**77 Ralph Vaughan Williams**     1872–1958   British
*Famous works:* Pastoral Symphony, Fantasia on
Greensleeves
*Style:* Operas, ballets, orchestral music, incidental, vocal,
chamber music
*Era:* Modern Times

**78 Sergei Rachmaninov**     1873–1943   Russian
*Famous works:* Rhapsody on a Theme of Paganini for Piano
and Orchestra, The Bells
*Style:* Orchestral, piano and choral
*Era:* Modern Times

**79 Arnold Schoenberg**     1874–1951   Austrian
*Famous works:* The Blessed Hand, The Transfigured Knight
*Style:* Operas, choral, orchestral, chamber and vocal
*Era:* Modern Times

**80 Charles Ives**   1874–1954   American
*Famous works:* The Circus Band, Three Places in New England, The Unanswered Question
*Style:* Orchestral, choral, chamber and piano
*Era:* Modern Times

**81 Maurice Ravel**   1875–1937   French
*Famous works:* Rapsodie Espagnole, Mother Goose
*Style:* Orchestral, piano, chamber music, song
*Era:* Modern Times

**82 Manuela de Falla**   1876–1946   Spanish
*Famous works:* The Three-cornered Hat, Atlantida
*Style:* Opera, ballet, choral and piano
*Era:* Modern Times

**83 Béla Bartók**   1881–1945   Hungarian
*Famous works:* Duke Bluebeard's Castle, The Wooden Prince, The Miraculous Mandarin
*Style:* Operas, ballets, orchestral, chamber and piano music
*Era:* Modern Times

**84 Igor Stravinsky**   1882–1971   Russian
*Famous works:* The Firebird, The Rite of Spring, Orpheus, The Soldier's Tale
*Style:* Operas, ballets, orchestral music, choral music
*Era:* Modern Times

**85 Anton Webern**   1883–1945   Austrian
*Famous works:* Passacaglia, Das Augenlicht
*Style:* Orchestral, choral, chamber and vocal
*Era:* Modern Times

**86 Edgard Varèse**   1883–1965   French/American
*Famous works:* Amériques, Hyperprism
*Style:* Orchestral, vocal, instrumental and electronic
*Era:* Modern Times

**87 Alban Berg**   1885–1935   Austrian
*Famous works:* Wozzeck, Lulu
*Style:* Opera, orchestral, chamber music, songs, piano music
*Era:* Modern Times

**88 Louis Durey**    1888–1979   French
*Famous work:* Le Printemps au fond de la mer
*Style:* Opera, instrumental and vocal music
*Notes:* One of 'Les Six'
*Era:* Modern Times

**89 Sergei Prokofiev**    1891–1953   Ukrainian
*Famous works:* The Gambler, War and Peace,
Romeo and Juliet
*Style:* Opera, ballets, orchestral, choral, chamber music,
piano music
*Era:* Modern Times

**90 Darius Milhaud**    1892–1974        French
*Famous work:* Les Malheurs d'Orphée
*Style:* Orchestral, choral, chamber and keyboard music
*Notes:* One of 'Les Six'
*Era:* Modern Times

**91 Germaine Tailleferre**    1892–1983   French
*Famous work:* 6 Chansons Françaises
*Style:* Opera, instrumental and vocal music
*Notes:* One of 'Les Six'
*Era:* Modern Times

**92 Arthur Honegger**    1892–1955   French
*Famous work:* Le Roi David
*Style:* Opera, ballet, orchestral and vocal music
*Notes:* One of 'Les Six'
*Era:* Modern Times

**93 Paul Hindemith**    1895–1963   German
*Famous works:* Matthias The Painter, The Four
Temperaments
*Style:* Operas, ballets, orchestral, chamber, piano, organ,
vocal, choral
*Era:* Modern Times

**94 Carl Orff**    1895–1982   German
*Famous work:* Carmina Burana
*Style:* Cantatas
*Era:* Modern Times

**95 Henry Cowell**  1897–1965  American
*Famous works:* Synchrony, Hymn and Fuguing Tune, Mosaic
*Style:* Orchestral, instrumental, piano
*Era:* Modern Times

**96 Francis Poulenc**  1899–1963  French
*Famous works:* A Sonata for Two Clarinets, Dialogues des
Carmélites
*Style:* Opera, instrumental and choral music
*Notes:* Leader of 'Les Six'
*Era:* Modern Times

**97 Georges Auric**  1899–1983  French
*Famous works:* Les Facheux, The Birds
*Style:* Opera, instrumental and choral music
*Notes:* One of 'Les Six'
*Era:* Modern Times

**98 Kurt Weill**  1900–1950  German
*Famous works:* The Threepenny Opera, The Knickerbocker
Holiday, The Rise and Fall of the City of Mahagonny
*Style:* Opera, ballet, orchestral, choral and chamber
*Era:* Modern Times

**99 Dmitri Shostakovich**  1906–1975  Russian
*Famous works:* The First of May, Leningrad, The Nose
*Style:* Orchestral, operas, chamber music and piano
*Era:* Modern Times

**100 Benjamin Britten**  1913–1976  British
*Famous works:* The Turn of the Screw, A Midsummer Night's
Dream, Variations on a Theme of Frank Bridge,
Spring Symphony
*Style:* Operas, church, orchestral, choral and chamber
*Era:* Modern Times

# The Writers 10

Writers are more than simply clever users of words. They may be more accurately described as investigators of *all* fields of human knowledge, using words as their major investigative tool.

When you explore the world of literature, you also explore the worlds of psychology, geography, philosophy, history, astronomy, economics, mathematics, politics, biology, physics, exploration, imagination and fantasy.

Thus, as you build up your Master Memory Matrix of the great writers, you will be simultaneously extending a multiplicity of associative grappling hooks into all realms of human knowledge. With every author and literary work you come to know, your ability to link with every other author and every other work will increase.

## Onword

This increase in knowledge will have as its automatic companions an increase in your speed of learning and an increase in your enjoyment of language, literature and life.

**1 Geoffrey Chaucer**    1340–1400    British
*Famous work:* The Canterbury Tales
*Educated:* London
*Notes:* Known as the 'Father of English Literature'

**2 Edmund Spenser**    1552–1599    British
*Famous works:* The Faerie Queene, Colin Clout's Come Home Againe
*Educated:* Merchant Taylors School, Northampton, then Cambridge
*Notes:* Often called 'Father of the English Fairytale'

**3 Sir Walter Raleigh**    1552–1618    British
*Famous works:* The History of the World, The Discoverie of the Large, Rich and Beautiful Empyre of Guiana
*Educated:* Oxford (Law)
*Notes:* An explorer and adventurer who led expeditions to America and South America. He had an enquiring mind and an uncommon literary ability

**4 Francis Bacon (Lord Verulam)**    1561–1626    British
*Famous work:* The Advancement of Learning
*Educated:* Trinity College, Cambridge (Law)
*Notes:* Had unquenchable curiosity about nature of the world and behaviour of his fellow men

**5 William Shakespeare**    1564–1616    British
*Famous works:* Othello, King Lear, Macbeth, Antony and Cleopatra, etc.
*Educated:* Holy Trinity Church, Stratford
*Notes:* Most prolific period 1604–1608. It is said of him that 'he is not of an age but for all time'

**6 Christopher Marlowe**    1564–1593    British
*Famous work:* The Passionate Shepherd
*Educated:* Corpus Christi College, Cambridge
*Notes:* Died from stabbing during fight with friends while gambling on backgammon

**7 John Donne**    1572–1631    British
*Famous works:* Devotions, Elegies and Sonnets
*Educated:* Oxford and Cambridge
*Notes:* One of the Metaphysical poets; became Dean of St Paul's in 1621 and wrote 160 sermons

**8 Ben Jonson**     1572–1637   British
*Famous works:* Volpone, Bartholomew Fayre, Timber
*Educated:* Westminster School
*Notes:* Leader of new generation of poets known as
'The Tribe of Ben'

**9 John Milton**     1608–1674   British
*Famous works:* Paradise Lost, On His Blindness, Il Penseroso
*Educated:* Christ's College Cambridge
*Notes:* The Civil War diverted his energies to the
parliamentary and political struggle. Wrote Paradise Lost
and On His Blindness after he had become blind

**10 John Bunyan**     1628–1688   British
*Famous works:* The Pilgrim's Progress, Grace Abounding
*Educated:* Village school, Elstow
*Notes:* He wrote The Pilgrim's Progress while imprisoned
for 12 years for unlicensed preaching

**11 John Dryden**     1631–1700   British
*Famous works:* Marriage à la Mode, The Rehearsal
*Educated:* Westminster School and Trinity College,
Cambridge
*Notes:* Poet Laureate in 1668

**12 Samuel Pepys**     1633–1703   British
*Famous work:* Diary
*Educated:* St Paul's School and Magdalene College, Cambridge
*Notes:* Diary not deciphered until 1825

**13 Daniel Defoe**     1660–1731   British
*Famous works:* Robinson Crusoe
*Educated:* Stoke Newington Academy
*Notes:* Most prolific after age of 60; dubbed 'founder of
English journalism'

**14 Jonathan Swift**     1667–1745   British
*Famous work:* Gulliver's Travels
*Educated:* Kilkenny School and Trinity College, Dublin
*Notes:* From age 23 suffered from Ménière's Disease

**15 Joseph Addison**     1672–1719   British
*Famous work:* Cato
*Educated:* Charterhouse School and Magdalen College,
Oxford
*Notes:* Member of Parliament

**16  George Berkeley**      1685–1753    Irish
*Famous works:* An Essay Towards a New Theory of Vision, Alciphron
*Educated:* Trinity College, Dublin
*Notes:* First published works were tracts on mathematics, written in Latin

**17  Alexander Pope**      1688–1744    British
*Famous works:* The Rape of the Lock and translations of The Iliad and Odyssey
*Educated:* Self-educated
*Notes:* Suffered from ill-health most of his life

**18  Samuel Richardson**      1689–1761    British
*Famous works:* Pamela, Clarissa
*Educated:* Grew up in poverty, education sketchy
*Notes:* Obsessed with sex, which led to the popularity of his writing. Regarded as 'one of the founders of the modern novel'

**19  Benjamin Franklin**      1706–1790    American
*Famous works:* Observation on the Relationships of Britain to her Colonies, Rules by which a Great Empire may be Reduced to a Small One
*Educated:* Born Boston, education sketchy
*Notes:* Scientist and politician; helped draft the American Constitution. Founded the influential social and debating society (The Junto Club)

**20  Henry Fielding**      1707–1754    British
*Famous works:* Tom Jones, The History of the Adventures of Joseph Andrews
*Educated:* Eton
*Notes:* Very sick much of his life with asthma and dropsy

**21  Samuel Johnson**      1709–1784    British
*Famous works:* Dictionary, The Vanity of Human Wishes
*Educated:* Pembroke College, Oxford
*Notes:* Famous lexicographer, critic and brilliant conversationalist and wit

**22  Thomas Gray**      1716–1771    British
*Famous work:* Elegy Written in a Country Churchyard
*Educated:* Eton and Peterhouse College, Cambridge
*Notes:* Letters are among finest in the language, incredible descriptive powers and wit

**23 Oliver Goldsmith**   1728–1774   Irish
*Famous works:* The Vicar of Wakefield, She Stoops to Conquer, The Citizen of the World
*Educated:* Trinity College, Dublin
*Notes:* In his own words, he was mostly addicted to gambling and was an experienced liar

**24 Edmund Burke**   1729–1797   Irish
*Famous work:* Reflections on the Revolution in France
*Educated:* Quakers School, Balitore, and Trinity College, Dublin
*Notes:* Whig politician and political theorist. Founded The Annual Register

**25 William Cowper**   1731–1800   British
*Famous works:* Table Talk, The Task
*Educated:* Westminster School, The Inner Temple (Law)
*Notes:* Trained as a lawyer and was converted to evangelical Christianity

**26 James Boswell**   1740–1795   Scottish
*Famous work:* The Life of Dr Johnson
*Educated:* Edinburgh University (Law)
*Notes:* Felt thwarted because he did not attain the political career he wanted

**27 Fanny Burney**   1752–1840   British
*Famous works:* Evelina, Cecilia, Camilla
*Educated:* Self-educated
*Notes:* Her diary is one of the best sources of first-hand portraits of late eighteenth-century characters and life

**28 George Crabbe**   1754–1832   British
*Famous work:* The Village
*Educated:* Apprentice to a doctor
*Notes:* Narrative poet of grim humour

**29 William Blake**   1757–1827   British
*Famous works:* Songs of Innocence and Experience, The Marriage of Heaven and Hell
*Educated:* Royal Academy at Somerset House
*Notes:* Volumes of meaning expressed in apparently simple musical lines of his poetry

**30 Robert Burns**    1759–1796   Scottish
*Famous works:* Tam-o'Shanter, Auld Lang Syne
*Educated:* By his father and mother
*Notes:* Wrote most remarkable cantata, The Jolly Beggar

**31 William Cobbett
('Peter Porcupine')**    1762–1835   British
*Famous works:* Rural Rides, Cobbett's Political Register,
Porcupine's Gazette
*Educated:* Self-educated in army
*Notes:* His published output was enormous, from farming
to politics

**32 William Wordsworth**    1770–1850   British
*Famous works:* Daffodils, Sonnets, Ode on the Intimations
of Immortality, Prelude
*Educated:* Hawkshead Grammar School and St John's
College, Cambridge
*Notes:* Born in the English Lake District; a leading Romantic
poet

**33 Sir Walter Scott**    1771–1832   Scottish
*Famous works:* Ivanhoe, Kenilworth
*Educated:* Royal High School and University in Edinburgh
*Notes:* Wrote almost 40 novels from 1814 to 1832

**34 Samuel Taylor Coleridge**    1772–1834   British
*Famous works:* Rime of the Ancient Mariner, Kubla Khan
*Educated:* Jesus College, Cambridge
*Notes:* Romantic poet who collaborated on Lyrical Ballads
with William Wordsworth; addicted to opium

**35 Jane Austen**    1775–1817   British
*Famous works:* Emma, Mansfield Park, Pride and Prejudice
*Educated:* By her father
*Notes:* Portrayed middle-class society with remarkable
subtlety

**36 Charles Lamb**    1775–1834   British
*Famous works:* Essays of Elia, Tales from Shakespeare
(written with his sister Mary)
*Educated:* Christ's Hospital
*Notes:* Devoted his life to his sister, who was mentally
unstable

**37 William Hazlitt**   1778–1830   British
*Famous works:* The Characters of Shakespeare's Plays
*Educated:* Hackney College, London (Art and Metaphysics)
*Notes:* Ability as a critic with remarkable physical
description through his observant artistic eye

**38 Thomas de Quincey**   1785–1859   British
*Famous works:* Confessions of an Opium-eater
*Educated:* Manchester Grammar School
*Notes:* Addicted to opium; work of uneven quality

**39 Lord George Gordon Byron**   1788–1824   British
*Famous works:* Manfred, Don Juan, Childe Harold
*Educated:* Aberdeen Grammar School, Harrow School,
Trinity College, Cambridge
*Notes:* Enormously influential Romantic poet who became
involved in Italian and Greek revolutionary politics

**40 James Fenimore Cooper**   1789–1851   American
*Famous works:* The Spy, The Last of the Mohicans
*Educated:* Albany and Yale
*Notes:* A judge

**41 Percy Bysshe Shelley**   1792–1822   British
*Famous works:* Prometheus Unbound, Ode to the West Wind
*Educated:* University College, Oxford
*Notes:* Leading figure in the Romantic movement; drowned
in Italy at age of 30

**42 John Clare**   1793–1864   British
*Famous works:* The Shepherd's Calendar, Poems Descriptive
of Rural Life and Scenery
*Educated:* By his father
*Notes:* Known as the Peasant Poet; spent much of his life in
an asylum

**43 John Keats**   1795–1821   British
*Famous works:* Hyperion, Ode to Autumn
*Educated:* Harrow School and Enfield Academy
*Notes:* Romantic poet who was apprenticed to an apothecary
and qualified for study of surgery at Guy's Hospital. Died of
tuberculosis at 26

**44 Thomas Carlyle**    1795–1881    Scottish
*Famous work:* Sartor Resartus
*Educated:* Annan Grammar School, Edinburgh University
*Notes:* Lost the use of his right hand and could no longer write

**45 Elizabeth Barrett Browning**    1806–1861    British
*Famous works:* The Cry of the Children, Sonnets from the
Portuguese, Aurora Leigh
*Educated:* At home
*Notes:* Married Robert Browning. She was recommended as
Poet Laureate

**46 Henry Wadsworth Longfellow**    1807–1882    American
*Famous works:* Song of Hiawatha, The Courtship of Miles
Standish
*Educated:* Bowdoin, Portland, Maine
*Notes:* First poems published at 13

**47 Edgar Allan Poe**    1809–1849    American
*Famous work:* The Pit and the Pendulum
*Educated:* University of Virginia
*Notes:* Trained as a lawyer. Stories often weird and fantastic

**48 Lord Alfred Tennyson**    1809–1892    British
*Famous works:* Maud, In Memoriam, The Eagle
*Educated:* Louth Grammar School and Trinity College,
Cambridge
*Notes:* Poet Laureate

**49 William Makepeace Thackeray**    1811–1863    British
*Famous works:* Vanity Fair, The Virginians
*Educated:* Trinity College, Cambridge (Law)
*Notes:* Studied law before becoming a journalist and
novelist. Travelled in the US and died at 52 of heartstrain

**50 Charles Dickens**    1812–1870    British
*Famous works:* Pickwick Papers, Oliver Twist, etc.
*Educated:* Intermittently
*Notes:* Novelist known for his memorable
characters and exposure of Victorian
social evils.

**51 Robert Browning**   1812–1889   British
*Famous works:* The Pied Piper of Hamelin, Home Thoughts
from Abroad
*Educated:* Mostly at home
*Notes:* Great romance of literary history with Elizabeth Barrett

**52 Anthony Trollope**   1815–1882   British
*Famous works:* The Barchester Chronicles,
The Way We Live Now
*Educated:* Harrow School
*Notes:* Clerk in the Post Office

**53 Charlotte Brontë**   1816–1855   British
*Famous work:* Jane Eyre
*Educated:* At a very harsh boarding school later portrayed
as Lowood in Jane Eyre
*Notes:* Taught in Brussels

**54 Emily Brontë**   1818–1848   British
*Famous work:* Wuthering Heights
*Educated:* At home in Haworth
*Notes:* Died of tuberculosis

**55 Charles Kingsley**   1819–1875   British
*Famous works:* The Water-Babies, Westward Ho!
*Educated:* King's College, London, and Magdalene College,
Cambridge
*Notes:* Deeply concerned with social reform but opposed
to change brought about by force

**56 George Eliot (Mary Ann Evans)**   1819–1880   British
*Famous works:* Silas Marner, Middlemarch
*Educated:* Privately at Coventry
*Notes:* Read extensively in theology and languages.
Left school following death of mother

**57 Walt Whitman**   1819–1892   American
*Famous work:* Leaves of Grass
*Educated:* Brooklyn
*Notes:* Led a wandering life and did hospital work during
the American Civil War

**58 John Ruskin**   1819–1900   British
*Famous work:* Modern Painters
*Educated:* By parents and at Christchurch, Oxford
*Notes:* Art critic and social reformer who laid the
foundations of the Arts and Crafts movement

**59  Anne Brontë**      1820–1849    British
*Famous work:* Agnes Grey
*Educated:* At home in Haworth
*Notes:* Used pseudonym Acton Bell. Died of tuberculosis
at age 29

**60  Matthew Arnold**      1822–1888    British
*Famous work:* Dover Beach
*Educated:* Rugby School and Balliol College, Oxford
*Notes:* Poet and critic

**61  Emily Dickinson**      1830–1886    American
*Famous work:* The Chariot
*Educated:* Amherst School and Academy, then Mount
Holyoke Female Seminary
*Notes:* America's greatest woman poet, who always wrote in
secret. Over 2000 poems discovered after her death

**62  Lewis Carroll**
**(Charles Lutwidge Dodgson)**      1832–1898    British
*Famous works:* Alice Through the Looking Glass,
Alice in Wonderland
*Educated:* Rugby School and Oxford (Maths)
*Notes:* A lecturer in mathematics at Oxford

**63  Mark Twain**
**(Samuel Langhorn Clemens)**      1835–1910    American
*Famous works:* Tom Sawyer, Huckleberry Finn
*Educated:* Left school at 12
*Notes:* Printer's apprentice and river pilot who became
leading American humourist

**64  Algernon Charles Swinburne**      1837–1909    British
*Famous works:* Atalanta in Calydon, Aeschylus and Sappho
*Educated:* Eton College and Balliol College, Oxford
*Notes:* His poetry often shocked with its eroticism

**65  Thomas Hardy**    1840–1928    British
*Famous works:* Far From the Madding Crowd, Tess of the
D'Urbervilles
*Educated:* Local schools in Dorset
*Notes:* Apprenticed to an architect, he became a novelist
and poet

**66 Henry James**   1843–1916   American
*Famous works:* The Turn of the Screw, The Wings of the Dove
*Educated:* Private tutors and part Law School
*Notes:* Europhile; prolific writings explored the Anglo-American gulf. Dense narrative sometimes difficult for readers to understand

**67 Gerard Manley Hopkins**   1844–1889   British
*Famous work:* The Wreck of the Deutschland
*Educated:* Balliol College, Oxford
*Notes:* Was an ordained priest and professor of Greek at University of Dublin. Felt conflict between poetry and religious calling. Died of typhoid

**68 Oscar Wilde**   1854–1900   Irish
*Famous works:* The Importance of Being Earnest, The Picture of Dorian Gray
*Educated:* Portora Royal School and Trinity College, Dublin, and Magdalen College, Oxford
*Notes:* Famous for wit and epigrammatic brilliance. Leader of the cult of 'Art for Art's sake'; imprisoned for homosexuality

**69 George Bernard Shaw**   1856–1950   Irish
*Famous works:* Man and Superman, Pygmalion
*Educated:* Left day school at 15
*Notes:* Became known as a journalist and critic and wrote nearly 60 plays. Letters edited by D H. Lawrence

**70 Joseph Conrad**   1857–1924   British
*Famous works:* Lord Jim, The Secret Agent, Under Western Eyes, Nostromo
*Educated:* Cracow, Poland
*Notes:* Born Polish Ukraine but exiled. Became a Master Mariner in British Merchant Navy. Wrote with clarity but never learnt to speak English well

**71 Sir Arthur Conan Doyle**   1859–1930   British
*Famous works:* Sherlock Holmes series
*Educated:* Edinburgh University (medicine)
*Notes:* A doctor who wrote short stories to supplement his income. Creator of the fictional character Sherlock Holmes. Worked as a senior physician in South Africa during the Boer War. Knighted in 1902

**72  J(ames) M(atthew) Barrie**     1860–1937   Scottish
*Famous work:* Peter Pan
*Educated:* By his mother, Dumfries Academy and Edinburgh University
*Notes:* The Boy David, his final play, awaits revival so that it can be properly judged on the stage

**73  W(illiam) B(utler) Yeats**     1865–1939   Irish
*Famous works:* Adoration of the Magi, The Wild Swans at Coole
*Educated:* London, Art School
*Notes:* Encouraged by his father, his Celtic inheritance was a powerful influence for him. Founded Dublin Hermetic Society to promote the study of Oriental religions and theosophy. Fell in love with Maude Gonne but she refused to marry him. He married a medium, Georgie Hyde-Lees, and they attempted 'automatic writing' with striking results

**74  Rudyard Kipling**     1865–1936   British
*Famous works:* Jungle Book, Just So Stories
*Educated:* United Services College, Devon
*Notes:* Born in Bombay, but left by family in London. Nobel Prize-winner in 1907

**75  H.G. (Herbert George) Wells**     1866–1946   British
*Famous works:* The Time Machine, Island of Dr Moreau, Wheels of Chance, Love and Mr Lewisham, Kipps
*Educated:* Royal College of Science, Kensington
*Notes:* Mixed scientific journalism with teaching. Wrote science fiction and fantasy stories side-by-side. Predicted many inventions that have come to pass

**76  John Galsworthy**     1867–1933   British
*Famous works:* The Forsyte Saga, The Silver Spoon, The Modern Comedy
*Educated:* Harrow School and New College, Oxford (Law)
*Notes:* Used pseudonym of John Sinjohn until after his fifth book. Wrote 31 full-length plays

**77  Arnold Bennett**     1867–1931   British
*Famous works:* The Old Wives' Tale, Clayhanger, Anna of the Five Towns, Riceyman Steps
*Educated:* Burslem Endowed School

*Notes:* Went to work for his father, a solicitor, at 18. Became a prolific journalist and novelist, setting much of his fiction in the Potteries district of Staffordshire

**78  Walter de la Mare**    1873–1956    British
*Famous works:* The Listeners
*Educated:* St Paul's Choir School
*Notes:* A poet, storyteller and novelist, whose work is characterised by an atmosphere of mystery. Wrote unpatronisingly for children, and continued to write into his eighties. Sometimes wrote under the name of Walter Ramal

**79  G(ilbert) K(eith) Chesterton**    1874–1936    British
*Famous works:* The Innocence of Father Brown, The Flying Inn
*Educated:* St Paul's School, Slade School of Art
*Notes:* Studied art, became a journalist and entered the Catholic Church in 1922

**80  William Somerset Maugham**    1874–1965    British
*Famous works:* Liza of Lambeth, Of Human Bondage
*Educated:* King's School, Canterbury and St Thomas' Hospital (Medicine)
*Notes:* Storyteller of genius with a sardonic view of human behaviour; anti-romantic and mercilessly observant, with an unrivalled skill in realising the climax of a story

**81  John Masefield**    1878–1967    British
*Famous works:* Salt-water Ballads, Reynard the Fox
*Educated:* King's School, Warwickshire
*Notes:* Went to sea but ill-health made him decide to become a writer

**82  E(dward) M(organ) Forster**    1879–1970    British
*Famous works:* The Longest Journey, A Room with a View, Where Angels Fear to Tread, Passage to India
*Educated:* Tonbridge School, King's College, Cambridge
*Notes:* Enjoyed exploring the contrast between 'buttoned-up' British culture and the warmer, more passionate cultures of other countries. Member of the Apostle Society, Chicago

**83  James Joyce**      1882–1969    Irish
*Famous works:* Ulysses, Finnegans Wake, Portrait of the
Artist as a Young Man
*Educated:* Jesuit School, Kildare, University College, Dublin
*Notes:* Ulysses published in serial form but was stopped as
obscene material

**84  D(avid) H(erbert) Lawrence**      1885–1930    British
*Famous works:* Sons and Lovers, Lady Chatterley's Lover
*Educated:* Nottingham High School
*Notes:* Tried to explore emotion and sexuality on a deep level.
Disharmony of home and parents strongly affected him

**85  Ezra Pound**      1885–1972    American
*Famous work:* The Spirit of Romance
*Educated:* University of Pennsylvania and Hamilton College,
New York
*Notes:* Travelled to Europe where he met writers, such as
T.S. Eliot, W.B. Yeats and Ernest Hemingway. His anti-
Semitism and sympathy with Mussolini led to his arrest and
subsequent confinement in an asylum until 1958

**86  Olaf Stapledon**      1886–1950    British
*Famous works:* Star Maker, Last and First Men, Last Men in
London, Sirius, A Man Divided
*Educated:* Abbotsholme School; Balliol College, Oxford;
Liverpool University
*Notes:* Father of modern science fiction and a freedom
fighter. University Lecturer in English Literature,
Psychology, Philosophy and Industrial History

**87  Edith Sitwell**      1887–1964    British
*Famous works:* Façade (set to music by William Walton),
Gold Coast Customs
*Educated:* At home
*Notes:* One of the most celebrated of English women,
awarded four honorary doctorates. 1948 Nobel Prize-winner

**88  Joyce Cary**      1888–1957    British
*Famous works:* Mister Johnson, The Horse's Mouth
*Educated:* Tonbridge Wells, Clifton College, Trinity College,
Oxford
*Notes:* Worked with the British Red Cross in the Balkan
Wars and as a District Magistrate in Nigeria. Wrote his first
novel at 44

**89 T(homas) S(tearns) Eliot**   1888–1965   British
*Famous works:* The Waste Land, The Four Quartets,
Old Possum's Book of Practical Cats (on which the musical
Cats was based)
*Educated:* Harvard University and Merton College, Oxford
*Notes:* The term 'Old Possum' was Ezra Pound's nickname for
Eliot and referred to his soft-footed, circuitous approach. Born
in St Louis, Missouri, he became a British subject in 1927

**90 Ivy Compton-Burnett**   1892–1969   British
*Famous work:* Pastors and Masters
*Educated:* Royal Holloway College, University of London
*Notes:* Her books deal with family relationships objectively
and unsentimentally

**91 J(ohn) B(oynton) Priestley**   1894–1984   British
*Famous works:* The Good Companions, Dangerous Corner
*Educated:* Trinity College, Cambridge
*Notes:* Wrote essays, literary criticism, travel, fiction,
autobiography and over 40 plays

**92 F(rancis) Scott Fitzgerald**   1896–1940   American
*Famous works:* Tender Is the Night, The Great Gatsby
*Educated:* Newman School, New Jersey, and Princeton
*Notes:* Led a life that epitomised the self-indulgence of the
'jazz age'. His glamorous wife Zelda suffered from mental
illness and he became a chronic alcoholic

**93 William Harrison Faulkner**   1897–1962   American
*Famous works:* The Sound and the Fury, As I Lay Dying
*Educated:* University of Mississippi
*Notes:* Won Pulitzer and Nobel Prizes. His novels provide
insight to a grim and complex era of American life

**94 Ernest Hemingway**   1898–1961   American
*Famous works:* A Farewell to Arms, For Whom the Bell
Tolls, The Old Man and the Sea
*Educated:* Oak Park School, Illinois
*Notes:* Known for 'masculine' writing style. 1954 Nobel
Prize-winner. Committed suicide

**95 Noël Coward**     1899–1973   British
*Famous works:* Private Lives, Blithe Spirit, Brief Encounter
*Educated:* Italia Conti Stage School
*Notes:* Successful actor and playwright. Flawless ear for spoken dialogue

**96 George Orwell**     1903–1950   British
*Famous works:* Animal Farm, 1984
*Educated:* Eton College
*Notes:* Served with Indian Civil Police in Burma, then returned to Europe as a teacher. Vivid commentator on reality of deprivation and became increasingly pessimistic about affairs at home and abroad

**97 Evelyn Waugh**     1903–1966   British
*Famous works:* Vile Bodies, Brideshead Revisited
*Educated:* Lancing School and Hertford College, Oxford
*Notes:* Worked as a teacher and a journalist

**98 C(ecil) Day Lewis**     1904–1972   British
*Famous works:* From Feathers to Iron, Overtures to Death
*Educated:* Sherborne School, Wadham College, Oxford
*Notes:* Poet Laureate and critic. Under pseudonym Nicholas Blake wrote 20 detective novels

**99 Graham Greene**     1904–1991   British
*Famous works:* The Heart of the Matter, Brighton Rock
*Educated:* Berkhamsted School, Balliol College, Oxford
*Notes:* Novelist, journalist and playwright. Awarded British Order of Merit in 1986

**100 Samuel Beckett**     1906–1987   Anglo-Irish
*Famous works:* Waiting for Godot, Malone Dies, Endgame
*Educated:* Trinity College, Dublin
*Notes:* Strongly associated with Theatre of the Absurd. Writings characterised by black humour and bleak interior monologues

# The Top 20 Geniuses of All Time

11

Genius is often thought to be a rare gift – something indefinable, something mysterious, and something that occurs only once in a lifetime.

In reality, genius is something quite different.

Genius is a range of mental qualities that can be measured and, more importantly, nurtured and grown (as you are doing with your own mental abilities in this book).

The standard qualities of genius include: Vision; Desire; Faith; Commitment; Planning; Persistence; Learning from mistakes; Subject knowledge; Mental Literacy; Imagination; Positive attitude; Auto-suggestion; Intuition; Real Master-Mind Group (Group of closest friends and advisors); Internal Master-Mind Group (Heroes, heroines and role models); Truth/honesty; Facing fears/courage; Creativity/flexibility; Love of the task; and Energy – Physical/sensual.

It will be useful to check your own development in these areas. Where you are strong you can continue to grow those strengths; where you are weak you can use your strengths to help make you stronger. Rank yourself out of 100 (0 = non-existent, 100 = perfect). Try to be as honest as possible, and retest yourself every few months.

In those geniuses who are defined as great by history, virtually all these qualities were developed to the maximum. How, then, can you discriminate between them? How can you assess the qualities of genius-within-genius?

Once again, there are measurable categories: dominance in the field of activity; active longevity; polymathy (skill and knowledge in many disciplines, as you are developing in *Master Your Memory*) and versatility; strength and energy; intelligence quotient; on-going influence on the development of the human race; prolificness; and achievement of prime goal. Add to these universality of vision, breakthrough originality; and a deliberate desire to pass on their new knowledge through teaching or academies, and a ranking becomes eminently possible. Tony Buzan, Grandmaster Raymond Keene, OBE, and a committee of international leaders in the fields of education, science, art, sport and Mind Sports, after years of impassioned discussion, settled on the rankings below. It may be interesting for you to devise your own list before memorising this one – see in what areas you agree with the compilers! (For more information on genius see *Buzan's Book of Genius*.)

## TOP 20 GENIUSES

|   | | Born | Died | Nationality | Area |
|---|---|---|---|---|---|
| 1 | Leonardo da Vinci | 1452 | 1519 | Italian | Artist/Inventor |
| 2 | William Shakespeare | 1564 | 1616 | British | Writer |
| 3 | Great Pyramid Builders | c. 2550 BC | | Egyptians | Architects |
| 4 | Johann Wolfgang von Goethe | 1749 | 1832 | German | Writer |
| 5 | Michelangelo | 1475 | 1564 | Italian | Artist |
| 6 | Sir Isaac Newton | 1642 | 1727 | British | Inventor |
| 7 | Thomas Jefferson | 1743 | 1826 | American | Politician |
| 8 | Alexander the Great | 356 BC | 323 BC | Macedonian | Monarch |
| 9 | Phidias | 500 BC | 432 BC | Greek | Artist |
| 10 | Albert Einstein | 1879 | 1955 | German | Scientist |
| 11 | Thomas Alva Edison | 1847 | 1931 | American | Inventor |
| 12 | Homer | Eighth century BC | | Greek | Writer |
| 13 | Plato | 428 BC | 348 BC | Greek | Philosopher |
| 14 | Euclid | c. 300 BC | | Greek | Teacher |
| 15 | Elizabeth I | 1533 | 1603 | British | Monarch |
| 16 | Archimedes | 287 BC | 212 BC | Greek | Scientist |
| 17 | Aristotle | 384 BC | 322 BC | Greek | Philosopher |
| 18 | Filippo Brunelleschi | 1377 | 1446 | Italian | Artist |
| 19 | Andrew Carnegie | 1835 | 1918 | Scottish | Industrialist |
| 20 | First Ch'in Emperor | 259 BC | 210 BC | Chinese | Monarch |

# Shakespeare
## The Complete Plays

 **Preview**
- The Greek Plays
- The Roman Plays
- English Historical Plays
- The Tragedies
- The Comedies
- The Moral Plays
- The Last Plays

The plays of William Shakespeare are regarded by many as the most comprehensive and masterful literary works in the English language, if not all languages. From them come an enormous number of the expressions and concepts we use today, and the names of many of the characters have become a major part of our cultural heritage.

Once you have a grasp of the basic plot and characters of Shakespeare's plays, you will be able to understand many other literary works more readily, to grasp more rapidly points being made in conversations, and to refer yourself, with sure knowledge, to Shakespearean events and characters. In addition to this, you will easily be able to unravel the 'who was related to whom, in what play, when and where?' conundrums with which so many people find themselves being faced. Rather than subsequently 'giving up' on Shakespeare because he is 'too confusing', you will be like a literary Sherlock Holmes, already hot on the trail of your informational goals.

One excellent method for using SEM$^3$ in conjunction with Shakespeare is to set aside an appropriate section of SEM$^3$

specifically for Shakespeare, and to memorise the basic plot and character for each play when you are about to see or hear it performed. We have set out the plays in such a way that there is a memorable quotation and chief characters to memorise as well as a summary of the plot. In this way, what you are memorising will be immediately relevant, will assist you with an understanding of the play by which you are about to be entertained, and will enable the play to assist you in the memorisation of itself! On the reverse side of this coin, you will find that using SEM$^3$ to help you memorise Shakespeare will encourage you to re-investigate the Bard, thus enhancing your social and cultural life.

Here is a list of the plays, in order of composition:

| | |
|---|---|
| 1589–92 | 1. *Henry VI*, 2. *Henry VI*, 3. *Henry VI* |
| 1592–93 | 4. *Richard III*, 5. *The Comedy of Errors* |
| 1593–94 | 6. *Titus Andronicus*, 7. *The Taming of the Shrew* |
| 1594–95 | 8. *The Two Gentlemen of Verona*, 9. *Love's Labour's Lost*, 10. *Romeo and Juliet* |
| 1595–96 | 11. *Richard II*, 12. *A Midsummer Night's Dream* |
| 1596–97 | 13. *King John*, 14. *The Merchant of Venice* |
| 1597–98 | 15. *Henry IV*, 16. *Henry IV* |
| 1598–99 | 17. *Much Ado About Nothing*, 18. *Henry V* |
| 1599–1600 | 19. *Julius Caesar*, 20. *As You Like It* |
| 1600–01 | 21. *Hamlet*, 22. *The Merry Wives of Windsor* |
| 1601–02 | 23. *Twelfth Night*, 24. *Troilus and Cressida* |
| 1602–03 | 25. *All's Well That Ends Well* |
| 1604–05 | 26. *Measure For Measure*, 27. *Othello* |
| 1605–06 | 28. *King Lear*, 29. *Macbeth* |
| 1606–07 | 30. *Antony and Cleopatra* |
| 1607–08 | 31. *Coriolanus*, 32. *Timon of Athens* |
| 1608–09 | 33. *Pericles* |
| 1609–10 | 34. *Cymbeline* |
| 1610–11 | 35. *The Winter's Tale* |
| 1611–12 | 36. *The Tempest* |
| 1612–13 | 37. *Henry VIII** |

The plays have been categorised in a new way to help with the understanding and memorisation of them. The Greek Plays, The Roman Plays, English Historical Plays, The Tragedies, The Comedies, The Moral Plays and The Last Plays.

---

* *The Tempest* is widely regarded as Shakespeare's final play. Although *Henry VIII* was completed later, it is thought to have been in collaboration with Fletcher and Beaumont.

# The Greek Plays

Unlike the Roman plays, Shakespeare's Greek plays do not fit any historical theme. They are essentially isolated stories taken from the Greek classical world. Of particular note is *Troilus and Cressida*, in which Shakespeare turns his hand to one of the most famous legends of all time, Homer's *Siege of Troy*.

### 1 • Pericles
### Prince of Tyre

Quote: *'Oh you gods! Why do you make us love your goodly gifts and snatch them straight away?'*

### *Dramatis Personae*

1  PERICLES, Prince of Tyre
2  CERIMON, a lord of Ephesus
3  MARINA, daughter to Pericles and Thaisa

This play is based upon the ancient tale of Apollonius of Tyre, a Greek romance. Pericles, who is a prince, loses his daughter and sets off on a long journey to regain her. He has many adventures, twice being shipwrecked. Eventually, with the help of Cerimon, a lord of Ephesus and also a physician, he finds her. The play may be summarised as: father has daughter; father loses daughter; father searches for daughter; father regains daughter.

### 2 • Timon of Athens

Quote: *'Men shut their doors against a setting sun.'*

### *Dramatis Personae*

1  TIMON of Athens

*Timon of Athens* is a biting satire on human ingratitude and disloyalty. The play starts with Timon as a wealthy man, a generous host and one who gives lavishly to his friends. Suddenly creditors demand repayment and he is bankrupt.

Timon sees this as a perfect opportunity for his friends to prove their brotherhood and justify his belief in the goodness of man. However, each friend turns him down, a shocking and cynical betrayal of Timon's trust in human nature. He becomes a disillusioned misanthropic hermit and dies in a tomb by the sea.

### 3 • Troilus and Cressida

Quote: *'Take but degree away, untune that string
and hark! what discord follows.'*

#### Dramatis Personae

1  HECTOR
2  TROILUS
3  PANDARUS, uncle to Cressida
4  AGAMEMNON, the Grecian general
5  ACHILLES
6  ULYSSES, Grecian commander
7  THERSITES, a deformed and scurrilous Grecian
8  CRESSIDA, daughter to Calchas
9  CALCHAS, father of Cressida and a Trojan priest
10  PARIS

*Troilus and Cressida* is Shakespeare's theatrical interpretation of
Homer's epic poem *The Iliad*. It recounts the siege of Troy, and the
refusal of the great hero Achilles to join in the siege because he has
been insulted by the Greek leader Agamemnon. The play chronicles
internal power struggles, the eventual return of Achilles to the war,
and his revenge against Hector, the hero of Troy. Against the
background of the ten-year war is set the story of Troilus and his
faithless lover Cressida. The play ends with the fall of Troy.

## The Roman Plays

Shakespeare's Roman plays span the entire pageant of Roman
history. *Coriolanus* details an epic moment from the Roman
Republic; *Julius Caesar* and *Antony and Cleopatra* depict the birth
pangs of the Roman Empire; while *Titus Andronicus* is set during
the Empire's decline and shows the accompanying collapse of
morals and political structures as the Empire loses its traditions
and direction under pressure from the Barbarians.

### 1 • Coriolanus

Quote: *'His nature is too noble for the world.'*

#### Dramatis Personae

1  CAIUS MARCIUS, afterwards CAIUS MARCIUS
   CORIOLANUS
2  TULLUS AUFIDIUS, general of the Volscians
3  VOLUMNIA, mother to Coriolanus
4  VIRGILIA, wife to Coriolanus

The story is a legend from the early days of the foundation of Rome's greatness. The general Coriolanus defeats Rome's chief enemy, the Volsces. He returns victorious to Rome expecting and expected to be made political as well as military leader. His arrogance, however, causes both the leaders and the population to rise against him. In revenge he joins the Volsces as their leader and vows to wreak havoc on Rome. At the last moment Volumnia and Virgilia, mother and wife of Coriolanus, persuade him not to attack Rome. As a result, the Volsces, considering him a traitor, assassinate Coriolanus.

### 2 ● Julius Caesar
Quote: *'Friends, Romans, Countrymen, lend me your ears.'*

### *Dramatis Personae*

1  JULIUS CAESAR, later as a GHOST
2  OCTAVIUS CAESAR
3  MARCUS ANTONIUS
4  MARCUS BRUTUS
5  CASSIUS
6  A SOOTHSAYER

*Julius Caesar* describes the early greatness and the assassination of the Roman dictator Caesar and sets the scene for an analysis of the foundation of the Roman Empire. The play recounts how Cassius and other conspirators plot to assassinate Julius Caesar and to make Brutus their leader. They stab Caesar to death on the Ides of March, as had been prophesied. Antony is given permission to speak at Caesar's funeral and, in a famous speech, rouses the crowds to fury at what has happened. The conspirators Cassius and Brutus raise armies, are defeated in battle and commit suicide.

### 3 ● Antony and Cleopatra
Quote: *'Age cannot wither her, nor custom stale her infinite variety.'*

### *Dramatis Personae*

1  MARK ANTONY
2  OCTAVIUS CAESAR
3  DOMITIUS ENOBARBUS
4  CLEOPATRA, Queen of Egypt
5  M. AEMILIUS LEPIDUS
6  OCTAVIA, sister to Caesar and wife to Antony

*Antony and Cleopatra* is the sequel to *Julius Caesar*. It tells how one of Caesar's chief lieutenants, Mark Antony, travels to Egypt to take over the eastern half of the Roman dominions. There he falls in love with Cleopatra, is obliged to return home, agrees to marry Octavia, Caesar's sister, but returns to Cleopatra in Egypt. Antony attempts to use Egypt as a base from which to take over the entire ancient Roman Empire. He is challenged by Octavius, Julius Caesar's nephew, who defeats him and rises to become the first Emperor Augustus. Having been defeated and hearing a false report that Cleopatra is dead, Antony commits suicide. Hearing of his death, Cleopatra similarly commits suicide, and the 'immortal' couple are buried together.

### 4 • Titus Andronicus

Quote: *'She is a woman, therefore may be wooed. She is a woman, therefore may be won.'*

#### *Dramatis Personae*

1 SATURNINUS, oldest son to the late Emperor of Rome, and afterwards declared EMPEROR
2 TITUS ANDRONICUS, a noble Roman, general against the Goths
3 TAMORA, Queen of the Goths
4 LAVINIA, daughter to Titus Andronicus

This play is academic, ambitious and masterfully planned, with a multiplicity of fearful events and climaxes. It begins in the late fourth century AD, during the gradual decline of the Roman Empire, when it is besieged by Goths. The great Roman general Titus kills the Gothic king, and continues the battle against the king's sons, but is gradually supplanted at Court by scheming rival factions. The play shows how he wreaks terrible revenge, including baking the sons of his enemies into a pie! Revenge complete, Titus commits suicide.

## English Historical Plays

Shakespeare's historical plays, apart from including some superb characters such as Sir John Falstaff and Prince Hal, detail a crucial period in English history, starting with the dethronement of King Richard II, covering Henry V's invasion of France in the Wars of the Roses, and culminating in the establishment of the Tudor dynasty. Queen Elizabeth I, one of Shakespeare's main patrons, was of course one of the main Tudor monarchs. The plays commence with the depiction of England in turmoil, pass through the brief military glory of Henry V, see the country plunged once again into chaos during the Wars of the Roses, and finally show order being triumphantly restored as the Tudor King Henry VII ascends the throne. The historical period covered is essentially 100 years, from 1385 to 1485. The sole exception in the historical pageant is the play *King John* which is separate from the sequence and rarely performed.

### 1 ● The Life and Death of King John

Quote: *'Come the three corners of the world in arms,*
*and we shall shock them.'*

#### *Dramatis Personae*

1  KING JOHN
2  PRINCE HENRY, son to the King
3  ARTHUR, Duke of Bretagne, nephew to the King
4  HUBERT DE BURGH
5  PHILIP THE BASTARD, his half-brother, later dubbed Richard Plantagenet
6  CARDINAL PANDULPH, the Pope's legate

This play explores the motives and behaviour of men competing for power. Events are concentrated around the fate of Arthur, and the foreshortening of the time scheme results in a dramatic intensification of the pressures in the conflict. John's corrupt greed for power is set against the ruthless fanaticism of Pandulph. Meanwhile Hubert and the Bastard move from cynicism and detachment to self-possession and integrity.

At the beginning of the play, John is seen as a fallible, uncertain, imperfect monarch, successful at first, and with his moment of glory in the full Protestant tradition as he confronts Pandulph. He is, however, increasingly subject to the corrupting power of political need, so that his final collapse is total.

### 2 ● The Tragedy of King Richard II

Quote: *'This happy breed of men, this little world, this precious stone*
*set in a silver sea . . . This England.'*

#### *Dramatis Personae*

1  KING RICHARD II
2  JOHN OF GAUNT, DUKE OF LANCASTER
3  HENRY, surnamed BOLINGBROKE, DUKE OF HEREFORD, son to John of Gaunt; afterwards KING HENRY IV

4  EARL OF NORTHUMBERLAND
5  SIR PIERCE OF EXTON

Richard II is a weak king who has failed to maintain England's military supremacy over her old enemy, France. Among Richard's unwise acts are the levying of various illegal taxes, and the confiscation of the property of John of Gaunt (Bolingbroke's father) on his death. As a consequence, Bolingbroke eventually overthrows Richard, who is sent to Pontefract, where he is murdered by Exton, who presents the body to Bolingbroke. He in turn feels remorse and goes on a crusade to atone for Richard's death. Bolingbroke eventually becomes King Henry IV.

### 3 ● The First Part of King Henry IV

Quote: *'What is honour? A Word – what is that word . . . Air.'*

### *Dramatis Personae*

1  KING HENRY THE FOURTH
2  HENRY, PRINCE OF WALES
3  HENRY PERCY, EARL OF NORTHUMBERLAND
4  HENRY PERCY, surnamed HOTSPUR, his son
5  SIR JOHN FALSTAFF
6  MISTRESS QUICKLY, hostess of a tavern in Eastcheap
7  THOMAS PERCY, EARL OF WORCESTER

Henry Bolingbroke, now the king, has trouble with his son Henry, Prince of Wales (Hal), who spends too much time in the tavern drinking with the 'low-life' Falstaff and getting involved in petty crime. Henry also has trouble with the Earl of Worcester, the Earl of Northumberland and his son, Hotspur, who plan a rebellion, culminating in the Battle of Shrewsbury. In the battle Prince Hal kills Hotspur, the plot being complicated by Falstaff who claims that it was he who did so. The play ends as King Henry prepares for the next battle, against still more conspirators.

### 4 ● The Second Part of King Henry IV

Quote: *'I am not only witty in myself, but the cause that wit is in other men.'*

### *Dramatis Personae*

1  KING HENRY IV
2  HENRY, PRINCE OF WALES afterwards KING HENRY V
3  LORD CHIEF JUSTICE of the King's Bench

4   SIR JOHN FALSTAFF
5   SHALLOW ⎫
                      ⎬ country justices
6   SILENCE ⎭
7   PRINCE JOHN OF LANCASTER
8   EARL OF NORTHUMBERLAND
9   SCROOP, ARCHBISHOP OF YORK

Rebellions continue, this time from the Archbishop of York and the Earl of Northumberland. The Archbishop is defeated by Prince John of Lancaster and the Earl of Northumberland is defeated by the Sheriff of Yorkshire.

After all the major rebellions have been put down, Henry eventually dies. Before he does he is reconciled with his son Hal, who develops from a riotous young prince into a just and wise ruler. His old friend Falstaff, now a knight, still gets into mischief but is no longer suitable company for the new King, who sends him to prison, but promises him a small pension.

### 5 ● The Life of King Henry V

Quote: *'Once more unto the breach dear friends, once more.'*

#### *Dramatis Personae*

1   KING HENRY V
2   PISTOL
3   LEWIS, THE DAUPHIN
4   KATHERINE, daughter to Charles and Isabel
5   DUKE OF BEDFORD, brother to the King
6   EARL OF SALISBURY
7   ARCHBISHOP OF CANTERBURY

The Archbishop of Canterbury advises the King that his descent from Isabella, the French Queen of Edward II, gives him the right to the French throne, and the Church would subsidise his going to war with France. Henry realises that this will also help to quell the internal disquiet from his own barons who are restless partly because Henry's own family is a usurper line.

The Dauphin mockingly sends Henry a box of tennis-balls in response to his claims to certain French dukedoms, so Henry promises war. The English take Harfleur but the army is weakened by disease and the French are much stronger. Henry encourages his soldiers and, against all odds, the French are defeated, and Henry takes the French throne. Henry develops into the model of a military monarch, and after the defeat of the French unites the Royal Houses by marrying Katherine, daughter of the French King.

## 6 ● The First Part of King Henry VI
Quote: *'From off this brier pluck a white rose with me.'*
*'Pluck a red rose from off this thorn with me.'*

### Dramatis Personae
1 KING HENRY VI
2 DUKE OF GLOUCESTER, uncle to the King and Lord Protector
3 HENRY BEAUFORT, BISHOP OF WINCHESTER, great-uncle to the King, afterwards CARDINAL
4 DUKE OF BEDFORD, uncle to the King and Regent of France
5 RICHARD PLANTAGENET, son of Richard late Earl of Cambridge, afterwards DUKE OF YORK
6 EARL OF SALISBURY
7 LORD TALBOT, afterwards Earl of Shrewsbury
8 CHARLES, Dauphin, and afterwards King, of France
9 DUKE OF BURGUNDY
10 MARGARET, daughter of Reignier, afterwards married to King Henry
11 JOAN LA PUCELLE, commonly called Joan of Arc

Henry V has died young, and his infant son Henry VI is technically on the throne. However, rival factions of barons now contend for mastery and the realm begins to weaken. The play deals with the multiple conflicts between the English and French. On the French side, Joan of Arc uses her persuasive powers to provoke the Duke of Burgundy's defection from the English cause.

The play ends with the seizure of Margaret of Anjou and Henry's betrothal to her, and with the Duke of York's capture of Joan and her trial and execution.

## 7 ● The Second Part of King Henry VI
Quote: *'Let's kill all the lawyers.'*

### Dramatis Personae
1 KING HENRY VI
2 HUMPHREY, DUKE OF GLOUCESTER, his uncle
3 CARDINAL BEAUFORT, BISHOP OF WINCHESTER, great-uncle to the King
4 JACK CADE, a rebel

The young Henry is now truly king, but the focus of the barons is on the quest for control. They fight among themselves, rather than defeating the ancient enemy France. The play shows a nation's abandonment of its vision and its social order. In this play Henry is defied by his wife, nobles and people; the rule of law breaks down; justice becomes a victim of whim and ambition; goodness is scorned in families and in the nation; and Christian virtue appears impotent when opposed by vigorous self-interest and violence.

The conditions necessary for correct rule are represented by King Henry and the Duke of Gloucester, Protector of the Realm. The play revolves around the reaction to the positive virtues of these two men. The Crown begins to totter.

### 8 • The Third Part of King Henry VI

Quote: *'Proud setter up and puller down of kings.'*

#### *Dramatis Personae*

1  KING HENRY VI
2  RICHARD PLANTAGENET, DUKE OF YORK
3  EDWARD, Earl of March, afterwards KING EDWARD IV
4  GEORGE, afterwards DUKE OF CLARENCE
5  RICHARD, afterwards DUKE OF GLOUCESTER
6  EARL OF WARWICK
7  QUEEN MARGARET

This play takes place during the 20-year period from 1455 to 1475, the time of the Wars of the Roses. The play focuses on the Duke of York, and his sons Edward, George and Richard, who plan to seize the throne from Henry VI of the House of Lancaster. England, still torn by internal strife and moral decay, is weakening; France is lost; and the Duke of York is killed in battle, although the House of York eventually triumphs. Henry VI is assassinated and the Duke of York's son Edward becomes king.

### 9 • The Tragedy of King Richard III

Quote: *'A horse, a horse, my kingdom for a horse.'*

#### *Dramatis Personae*

1  KING EDWARD IV
2  RICHARD, DUKE OF GLOUCESTER,
   afterwards KING RICHARD III

3  HENRY, EARL OF RICHMOND,
   afterwards KING HENRY VII
4  DUKE OF BUCKINGHAM, later as a GHOST

With Edward IV now king, Richard, Duke of Gloucester, the Duke of York's youngest son, plots to seize the throne. His problem lies in the fact that he is fifth in the line of succession.

The play follows his machiavellian practices as he assassinates every single possible rival claimant, including, in a famous scene, the two young princes. He eventually becomes king and plans to marry Edward's daughter Elizabeth.

At the end of the play, having become king, his evil deeds catch up with him. The ghosts of all Richard's victims appear and prophesy his death. He is overthrown by Henry, Earl of Richmond, at the Battle of Bosworth. Henry becomes King Henry VII and unites the Houses of York and Lancaster, the groups of previously contending barons. Peace reigns.

### 10 ● The Famous History of the Life of King Henry VIII

Quote: *'In her days everyman shall eat in safety under his own vine . . . and sing the merry songs of peace to all his neighbours.'*

### *Dramatis Personae*

1  KING HENRY VIII
2  CARDINAL WOLSEY
3  DUKE OF BUCKINGHAM
4  QUEEN KATHARINE, wife to King Henry,
   afterwards divorced
5  ANNE BULLEN, her Maid of Honour, afterwards Queen

This is Shakespeare's only play to be entitled a 'Famous History' and takes unusual care to be historically accurate. The play's form is wave-like, with great swells of events bearing the King and leading figures upward and downward, to and from high places.

The Duke of Buckingham, having decided to challenge the overbearing Wolsey, is arrested before he can take measures either of attack or defence. Queen Katharine demonstrates her courage by speaking for him and against Cardinal Wolsey; Buckingham is executed. Meanwhile the King starts to raise Anne Boleyn (Bullen) to the throne, as Katharine falls from grace and there is a divorce trial. Then even Wolsey is convicted of exorbitant gains and falls from power. To counter-balance this, Anne is crowned and

Princess Elizabeth is born. *Henry VIII* finishes in a triumphant mood and is clearly meant to celebrate the reign.

By this time Henry and Anne Boleyn have produced a daughter who eventually becomes Queen Elizabeth. The play is essentially a hymn of praise to the Tudor dynasty and to Queen Elizabeth who was, of course, on the throne while Shakespeare was writing this play.

## The Tragedies

In his tragedies Shakespeare adopts the classical Greek definition of tragedy put forward by Aristotle in his *Poetics* – they all show a great man brought to a tragic end through the ineluctable workings of a fatal flaw. The flaw, in some circumstances, could be considered a strength, but as the plays develop it always turns out to be an Achilles' heel. For example, Macbeth's ambition is a great driving force in his career, but, taken to excess, it leads to his downfall. With Lear, the tragic flaw is pride; in Othello, it is jealousy (though it was Othello's enormous possessiveness towards Desdemona that led to his gaining such a brilliant wife in the first place); while with Hamlet it is indecision. Seeing both sides of every argument and questioning the validity of your own motives can be a strength but Hamlet takes it too far.

### 1 ● Macbeth
Quote: *'Double, double, toil and trouble;*
*fire burn and cauldron bubble.'*

#### Dramatis Personae
1  MACBETH
2  BANQUO ⎫
3  MACDUFF ⎬ generals of the King's army
4  LADY MACBETH
5  THREE WITCHES
6  DUNCAN, King of Scotland
7  FLEANCE, son to Banquo

*Macbeth* takes ambition as its central pillar, as *King Lear* takes pride. The play recounts the rise of the Scottish nobleman Macbeth in the 11th century AD from leading chieftain in Scotland, through various bloody deeds, towards kingship. Egged on by both his wife and by mystical powers, he commits murder after murder, but is finally overcome by the forces of righteousness.

Three witches prophesy that Macbeth will be king and Banquo will be father to a line of kings. Lady Macbeth urges her husband to murder the King. Macbeth is crowned and, to stop the witches' prophecy being fulfilled, he hires murderers to kill Banquo and his son Fleance, but Fleance escapes. Macbeth sees the ghost of Banquo and he seeks out the witches who tell him to beware of Macduff, and repeat that descendants of Banquo will become kings.

Macbeth has Macduff's wife and children murdered; Macduff and his men besiege Macbeth's castle. Lady Macbeth commits suicide, Macduff kills Macbeth, and Malcolm, the eldest son of Duncan, becomes King.

### 2 ● Othello, the Moor of Venice

Quote: *'Oh beware, my Lord, of jealousy It is the green-eyed monster which doth mock the meat it feeds on.'*

### *Dramatis Personae*

1  OTHELLO, a noble Moor in the service of the
   Venetian state
2  CASSIO, his lieutenant
3  IAGO, his servant
4  RODERIGO, a Venetian gentleman
5  DESDEMONA, daughter to Brabantio and wife to Othello
6  BIANCA, mistress to Cassio

*Othello* is considered by many to be Shakespeare's most personal play. It shows the marriage between the black Arab or Moor, Othello, and the white Italian Renaissance virgin Desdemona. Iago and Roderigo, in love with Desdemona, plot against Othello and his lieutenant, Cassio, by making Othello suspect Desdemona and Cassio of adultery. At the close, Othello kills Desdemona, but then realises he has been misled by his evil servant Iago. Filled with guilt and remorse, he kills himself.

The speed with which Othello becomes insanely jealous and the pressure and the violence of his emotions, have led many critics to believe that these were emotions that Shakespeare had personally experienced.

### 3 ● King Lear

Quote: *'How sharper than a serpent's tooth it is to have a thankless child.'*

#### *Dramatis Personae*

1  LEAR, King of Britain
2  FOOL
3  GONERIL ⎫
4  REGAN   ⎬ daughters to Lear
5  CORDELIA ⎭

*King Lear*, like *Cymbeline*, takes ancient Britain as its stage. The king, Lear, retires and divides his kingdom between two of his daughters, Regan and Goneril, who have won favour with him through flattery. As in *Timon of Athens*, the theme of ingratitude emerges, as the daughters compete for dominance, reject Lear, and cast him out.

Lear's other daughter, Cordelia, is married to the King of France without a dowry. Having refused to flatter her father, she has been cut out of Lear's division of the kingdom. Hearing of his plight, Cordelia brings an army from France to rescue him, but she is murdered. Lear, with the daughter to whom he had been unkind and who had tried to rescue him dead, and with those to whom he had given everything now rejecting him, goes mad and perishes.

### 4 ● Hamlet
### Prince of Denmark

Quote: *'To be or not to be. That is the question.'*

#### *Dramatis Personae*

1   CLAUDIUS, King of Denmark
2   HAMLET, son to the late, and nephew to the present, King
3   POLONIUS, Lord Chamberlain
4   HORATIO, friend to Hamlet
5   LAERTES, son to Polonius
6   TWO CLOWNS, gravediggers
7   GHOST of Hamlet's father
8   GERTRUDE, Queen of Denmark, and mother to Hamlet
9   OPHELIA, daughter to Polonius
10  ROSENCRANTZ ⎫
               ⎬ Courtiers
11  GUILDENSTERN ⎭
12  FORTINBRAS, Prince of Norway

*Hamlet* is a revenge tragedy in which a wronged son seeks revenge against those who have committed crimes, in this case the murder of his father and the 'theft' of the crown of Denmark. What adds eternal lustre to this particular theme is that Hamlet is too intelligent to simply carry out the acts of revenge, and constantly questions his own motives. Ultimately he goes too far in questioning, and obscures rather than clarifies the situations he's trying to resolve.

Hamlet is told by the ghost of his father that he was murdered by his brother Claudius, now King. Hamlet feigns madness while plotting revenge. He organises a play depicting his father's death to confirm Claudius' guilt. While warning his mother, Hamlet kills Polonius, who is eavesdropping. Claudius sends Hamlet to England to be killed but he escapes and returns to Denmark.

Ophelia, Polonius' daughter, once loved by Hamlet, has drowned herself. The King proposes a duel between Hamlet and the son of Polonius, Laertes. Hamlet is wounded by a poisoned sword which he then takes to kill Laertes and the King. The Queen drinks poisoned wine prepared for Hamlet, and Hamlet dies from his own wound.

# The Comedies

Shakespeare's comedies are heavily based on the standard Italian form of the *Commedia del Arte*, frequently involving twins, lookalikes, brothers and sisters, cross-dressing and mistaken identities. Naturally Shakespeare injects his own element of genius into the pre-existing plots.

### 1 ● The Comedy of Errors

Quote: *'Am I in Earth, in Heaven or in Hell, sleeping or waking, mad or well advised?'*

### Dramatis Personae

1  SOLINUS, DUKE OF EPHESUS
2  AEGEON, a merchant of Syracuse
3  ANTIPHOLUS OF EPHESUS ⎫ twin brothers, and sons
4  ANTIPHOLUS OF SYRACUSE ⎭ of Aegeon and Aemilia
5  DROMIO OF EPHESUS ⎫ twin brothers, and attendants
6  DROMIO OF SYRACUSE ⎭ on the two Antipholuses
7  AEMILIA, wife to Aegeon, an abbess at Ephesus
8  ADRIANA, wife to Antipholus of Ephesus
9  LUCIANA, her sister

*The Comedy of Errors*, based on Plautus's *Menaechmi*, is a delightful tale of twins, more twins, brothers and sisters, wives and lovers, all of whom become intriguingly intertwined in a series of playful misidentifications and misunderstandings.

The play primarily revolves around the two Antipholus twins, one of whom wanders away from home as a boy, and whose father consequently dies of grief.

The boy lives, grows up and marries, and the story begins with him having stolen his wife's cloak to give to his mistress. At the same time his brother arrives, looking for his lost twin.

At this point, the mistress mistakes the twin for her lover and the plot becomes wonderfully complex, with the brother having the cloak, and also meeting his brother's wife. When the original brother returns he is locked out of both his lover's and his wife's houses. However, just in time, the two brothers are seen together and the reason for the confusion is evident. They are happily reunited and go to live in Syracuse.

### 2 ● The Taming of the Shrew

Quote: *'For I am he am born to tame you, Kate, and bring you from a wild Kate to a Kate conformable as other household Kates.'*

#### *Dramatis Personae*

1 BAPTISTA MINOLA, a rich gentleman of Padua
2 PETRUCHIO, a gentleman of Verona, a suitor to Katharina
3 KATHARINA, the shrew ⎫
　　　　　　　　　　　　　⎬ daughters to Baptista
4 BIANCA ⎭
5 LUCENTIO, son to Vincentio, in love with Bianca

A satire on relationships between men and women. Bianca is not allowed to marry until her bad-tempered elder sister, Kate, is married. Her father, Baptista, looks for tutors for Bianca and suitors for Katharina. The young Lucentio falls in love with Bianca, disguises himself as a tutor, and they secretly elope.

Kate is a frightful shrew who beats every man she meets into submission and refuses to entertain even the idea of marriage. Petruchio, a gentleman of Verona, who is prepared to marry anyone for money, gradually 'tames' Kate in a series of what might now be considered quite chauvinistic manoeuvres. At the end of the play the two achieve marital balance and harmony.

### 3 ● The Two Gentlemen of Verona

Quote: *'How use doth breed a habit in a man.'*

#### *Dramatis Personae*

1  DUKE OF MILAN, father to Silvia
2  VALENTINE ⎫
3  PROTEUS    ⎬ the two Gentlemen
4  ANTONIO, father to Proteus
5  JULIA, beloved of Proteus
6  SILVIA, beloved of Valentine

*The Two Gentlemen of Verona* is a standard romance, where love is subjected to strain from without and within. Antonio, father of Proteus, demands that his son separate from his mistress, and then Antonio falls prey to a momentary sensual attraction.

Valentine, the other 'gentleman', is banished by the duke for 'indiscreet' behaviour. The play focuses on the conflict between the men created by the demands of friendship and their various sexual attractions. After increasing difficulties, Valentine finally restores Proteus to his own favour, even offering him his own mistress.

### 4 ● Love's Labour's Lost

Quote: *'They have been at a great feast of languages and stolen the scraps.'*

#### *Dramatis Personae*

1  FERDINAND, KING OF NAVARRE
2  BEROWNE     ⎫
3  LONGAVILLE  ⎬ lords attending on the King
4  DUMAIN      ⎭
5  THE PRINCESS OF FRANCE
6  ROSALINE    ⎫
7  MARIA       ⎬ ladies attending on the Princess
8  KATHARINE   ⎭

Ferdinand, King of Navarre, persuades three of his courtiers, Berowne, Longaville and Dumain, to abstain from the company of women for three years. But the arrival of a French Princess and her entourage causes problems, as they each fall in love: Berowne with Rosaline; the King with the Princess; Longaville with Maria; and Dumain with Katharine.

Love poems are sent and tricks are played, but news of the French King's death necessitates the ladies' return to France. They promise that, after their period of mourning, they will return if, in between, the four men spend their time doing good deeds.

## 5 ● A Midsummer Night's Dream

Quote: *'Methought I was enamour'd of an ass.'*

### *Dramatis Personae*

1 THESEUS, Duke of Athens
2 LYSANDER
3 DEMETRIUS } in love with Hermia
4 BOTTOM, a weaver
5 HERMIA, daughter to Egeus, in love with Lysander
6 HELENA, in love with Demetrius
7 OBERON, King of the fairies
8 TITANIA, Queen of the fairies
9 PUCK, or Robin Goodfellow
10 HIPPOLYTA, Queen of the Amazons, betrothed to Theseus

*A Midsummer Night's Dream* is a witty examination of the mysterious relationships between men and women. It shows how love can be both rational and irrational at the same time.

Theseus, Duke of Athens, is to marry Hippolyta, Queen of the Amazons. Hermia refuses to give up her lover, Lysander, to marry Demetrius, and they flee to a wood, pursued by Demetrius. Demetrius, in turn, is followed by Helena, whom he has slighted in love.

In the wood, a lot of tomfoolery goes on, with Oberon casting spells on Titania and Puck playing tricks on Bottom. The play shows how romantic affections can attach themselves to the most ridiculous objects, as when Titania falls in love with an ass, who is really Bottom in disguise.

As the play ends, the magical threads are unravelled, reality returns, and all the characters go back to Athens for a triple wedding, at which the play *Pyramus and Thisbe* is enacted.

## 6 ● Much Ado About Nothing

Quote: *'For there was never yet philosopher who could endure the toothache patiently.'*

## *Dramatis Personae*

1  DON PEDRO, Prince of Aragon
2  DON JOHN, his bastard brother
3  BENEDICK, a young lord of Padua
4  DOGBERRY, a constable
5  LEONATO, Governor of Messina
6  BEATRICE, niece to Leonato
7  HERO, daughter to Leonato
8  CLAUDIO, a young lord of Florence

*Much Ado About Nothing* is a comedy of manners. Don Pedro, Prince of Aragon, and two friends, Claudio and Benedick, stay in Messina with Leonato, the Governor. Don Pedro agrees to woo Leonato's daughter, Hero, on Claudio's behalf. Meanwhile Don Pedro, Leonato and Claudio plot to bring Beatrice, Leonato's niece, and Benedick together.

Hero is alleged to be unfaithful and Claudio denounces her, but the conspirators who planned this are discovered. For distrusting Hero, Benedick and Leonato both challenge Claudio to a duel but Claudio repents. All ends well and there is a double wedding: Claudio and Hero, Beatrice and Benedick.

The play could be said to revolve around Beatrice and Benedick, who, although under the surface deeply in love, spend most of their time squabbling and using their sharp wits at each other's expense. However, when the petty squabblings and 'nothing' threaten to become a real danger to their community, they put aside their differences and are happily united.

## 7 ● As You Like It

Quote: *'All the world's a stage and all the men and women merely players.'*

### *Dramatis Personae*

1  DUKE SENIOR, living in banishment
2  FREDERICK, his brother and usurper of his dominions
3  JAQUES, a banished duke
4  TOUCHSTONE, a clown
5  ROSALIND, daughter to the banished Duke
6  CELIA, daughter to Frederick

*As You Like It* is a charming rustic comedy in which a deposed duke, Senior, living in the forest as an outcast, hopes to reunite various lovers. In witty political and family intrigues, the lovers assume various disguises, including that of Rosalind who disguises herself as a man, causing all sorts of humorous complications. After much hilarious confusion, so typical of Shakespeare, the real relationships are all clarified, true love finds a way, and the play ends with four weddings.

### 8 ● The Merry Wives Of Windsor

Quote: *'The world's mine oyster.'*

#### Dramatis Personae

1 SIR JOHN FALSTAFF
2 FENTON, a gentleman
3 FORD ⎱
4 PAGE ⎰ two gentlemen dwelling at Windsor
5 MISTRESS FORD
6 MISTRESS PAGE
7 MISTRESS QUICKLY, servant to Doctor Caius

It is said that Shakespeare wrote this play because Queen Elizabeth I was so charmed by the old rogue Falstaff in the *Henry IV* plays that she demanded a reappearance. The story is about life in the comfortable, self-assured community of Windsor where daughters Page and Ford, enterprising and independent young women, are actively involved in seeking husbands. Enter Falstaff, who arrives short of funds as usual and attempts to earn some necessary cash by means of the wives of various local citizens. Like many of Shakespeare's comedies, the play interweaves the multiple threads of relationships, involving all the representative characters of the community: two professional men, a doctor and a parson, the host of the inn and a born gossip.

The play recounts false jealousies on the part of husbands who think they are being cuckolded. Falstaff is eventually thrown into the river in a laundry basket and becomes the butt of their humour, wearing a pair of antlers (cuckold's horns) in a midnight ceremony in Windsor forest.

### 9 ● Twelfth Night
### Or, What You Will

Quote: 'Some *men are born great, some achieve greatness and some have greatness thrust upon them.'*

## *Dramatis Personae*

1  ORSINO, DUKE OF ILLYRIA
2  OLIVIA
3  VIOLA
4  SEBASTIAN, brother to Viola
5  SIR TOBY BELCH, uncle to Olivia
6  SIR ANDREW AGUECHEEK
7  MALVOLIO, steward to Olivia
8  FESTE, A CLOWN

Like *The Two Gentlemen of Verona* and *A Midsummer Night's Dream*, *Twelfth Night* is a comedy of manners in which various lovers go through mistaken identities and multiple confusions. In the play certain types of people are held up for ridicule, such as Malvolio, the pompous servant, who takes life far too seriously and ends up being imprisoned and tormented by what he thinks are ghosts. We also see conniving servants, lords who believe themselves to be in love, and ladies who are in love with the 'wrong' person.

*Twelfth Night* also includes a Falstaffian character in the person of Sir Toby Belch, a hard-drinking, duelling roisterer. As with all Shakespeare's comedies, the play ends with everything happily resolved and all the characters going merrily on their way.

## 10 ● All's Well That Ends Well

Quote: *'They say miracles are past.'*

## *Dramatis Personae*

1  KING OF FRANCE
2  BERTRAM, Count of Rousillon
3  COUNTESS OF ROUSILLON, mother to Bertram
4  HELENA, a gentlewoman protected by the Countess

This play, the last of Shakespeare's comedies, actually marks a transition between the comedy plays and the moral plays, and is often thought of as a 'dark comedy' or 'problem play'. It is full of issues that can tax and vex the mind. It is a love story, although not full of happiness. It does, however, end as well as it can. Helena is rejected by Bertram on the grounds of her inferior class, while the King speaks rationally and passionately about the value of merit over birth.

The scene begins with Helena beginning her 'cure'. This is a 'bed trick' where she must trick her husband into making love to her without him knowing it is her. This she does, but although she becomes pregnant, he loves the 'shadow' of her and there is no firm close or resolution.

## The Moral Plays

Not pure comedies, not pure tragedies, but with elements of both. In these plays moral dilemmas are explored, confronting the audience with the question: 'What would I do in this situation?'

### 1 ● Romeo and Juliet

Quote: *'Oh Romeo, Romeo, wherefore art thou Romeo?'*
*'What's in a name? That which we call a rose by any other name would smell as sweet.'*

#### *Dramatis Personae*

1  PARIS, a young nobleman
2  MONTAGUE ⎤ heads of two houses at
3  CAPULET ⎦ variance with each other
4  ROMEO, son to Montague
5  MERCUTIO, friend to Romeo
6  TYBALT, nephew to Lady Capulet
7  FRIAR LAURENCE, Franciscan
8  JULIET, daughter to Capulet
9  NURSE to Juliet

Two rival families, the Montagues and the Capulets, vie for pre-eminence in Renaissance Italy.

Paris, a young nobleman, has asked to marry Juliet, Capulet's 13-year-old daughter, but has been told that she is far too young.

Romeo, the son of Montague, goes to a Capulet party in disguise, and meets Juliet. They fall in love and secretly get married, but Romeo is banished after a family fight in which his friend Mercutio and the Capulet Tybalt are killed.

Amid the growing tension, Capulet changes his mind and insists that Paris and Juliet must be married within two days. Distraught but cleverly scheming, Juliet takes a potion which gives her the appearance of death. Romeo, discovering her, believes that she is dead and poisons himself. On waking, Juliet discovers the dead Romeo by her side and kills herself. The tragedy of their untimely deaths finally reconciles the families and brings peace to the town.

### 2 ● The Merchant of Venice

Quote: *'The quality of mercy is not strained.*
*It droppeth as the gentle rain from heaven.'*

### *Dramatis Personae*

1  ANTONIO, a merchant of Venice
2  SHYLOCK, a rich Jew
3  JESSICA, daughter to Shylock
4  LORENZO, in love with Jessica
5  BASSANIO, Lorenzo's friend, suitor to Portia
6  PORTIA, a rich heiress
7  NERISSA, Portia's maid

*The Merchant of Venice* is essentially a disquisition on the theme of mercy and compassion in human relationships.

To try to win the hand of Portia, Bassanio borrows money from his friend Antonio, who has to borrow that money from Shylock, a Jewish money-lender. Antonio agrees that, if it is not repaid within three months, Shylock can remove a pound in weight from Antonio's flesh.

Shylock's daughter, Jessica, elopes with Lorenzo, a Gentile, and Bassanio marries Portia.

Antonio's ships run aground, which means he cannot repay his loan. Shylock demands his pound of flesh. Disguised as a young lawyer and clerk, Portia and Nerissa, her maid, win Antonio's case in court. Shylock loses all and, on Antonio's insistence, becomes a Christian. Antonio's ships are happily saved.

### 3 • Measure for Measure

Quote: *'Liberty plucks justice by the nose.'*

### *Dramatis Personae*

1  VINCENTIO, the Duke
2  ANGELO, the Deputy
3  CLAUDIO, a young gentleman
4  ISABELLA, sister to Claudio
5  MARIANA, betrothed to Angelo

*Measure for Measure* is a subtle investigation into the nature of justice and whether or not justice is absolute or can be tempered with mercy. It holds up a revealing mirror to human nature.

In the play Duke Vincentio leaves his deputy, Angelo, in charge of Vienna, but disguises himself as a friar in order to keep an eye on things. Angelo starts a vindictive 'clean-up' campaign, including sentencing a young gentleman, Claudio, to the death penalty for fornication.

Isabella, Claudio's sister, who is about to enter a nunnery, pleads with Angelo to have mercy.

Angelo falls madly in love with Isabella, and offers to spare Claudio if she will give herself to him. The 'friar' has, however, been observing all these events. At his suggestion, Isabella only pretends to accept Angelo's proposal, but sends Mariana, who is already betrothed to Angelo, in her place.

Angelo, increasingly corrupted by his power, does not keep his promise and still orders Claudio's execution. The 'moral' characters arrange for a pirate to be substituted for Claudio, and the 'returned' Duke condemns Angelo to death. Finally, showing extreme mercy, the Duke pardons both Angelo and Claudio and, having fallen in love with Isabella, while disguised as the friar, asks her to marry him.

## The Last Plays

Shakespeare progresses from the view expressed in his earlier masterpieces that tragic events must always have tragic outcomes. His final plays are characterised by intelligent and humane solutions to 'at first sight' disastrous situations.

### 1 ● Cymbeline
### King of Britain

Quote: *'Fear no more the heat of the sun nor
the furious winter's rages.'*

#### Dramatis Personae

1  CYMBELINE, King of Britain
2  CLOTEN, son to the Queen by a former husband
3  POSTHUMUS LEONATUS, a gentleman, husband to Imogen
4  IMOGEN, daughter to Cymbeline by a former Queen
5  BELARIUS, a banished lord disguised under the name of Morgan
6  GUIDERIUS ⎫ sons to Cymbeline
7  ARVIRAGUS ⎭
8  QUEEN, wife to Cymbeline

This play is set during a period when Britain was essentially no longer part of the Roman Empire but was rising as a power almost equal to that of Rome. Cymbeline opposes his daughter Imogen's marriage to Posthumus; as a result, Posthumus is banished to Italy. The Queen plots to take control of the country from Cymbeline and make Cloten, her son, king, with Imogen as his bride. She successfully schemes to have the Romans declare war on Britain.

Through the Queen's conniving, Posthumus comes to believe that Imogen has been unfaithful, and orders her killed; fortunately he is unsuccessful.

The plot thickens at the arrival of Belarius, who has lived for years in a cave after kidnapping Guiderius and Arviragus, sons of Cymbeline. In the ensuing battles Guiderius kills Cloten, the Romans are defeated and peace is restored.

In the final scenes Posthumus repents and is reconciled with Imogen; the evil Queen dies; and the King is happily reunited with his sons.

### 2 ● The Winter's Tale

Quote: *'Exit pursued by a bear.'*

#### *Dramatis Personae*

1  LEONTES, King of Sicilia
2  AUTOLYCUS, a rogue
3  HERMIONE, Queen to Leontes
4  PERDITA, daughter to Leontes and Hermione
5  POLIXENES, King of Bohemia
6  FLORIZEL, Prince of Bohemia

*The Winter's Tale* has some similarities to *Othello*. Both plays involve the theme of jealousy and a powerful man who believes his wife to be unfaithful.

In this play, the King, Leontes, believes Hermione, his wife, and Polixenes, his friend and the King of Bohemia, are having an affair. As his suspicions increase, Leontes imprisons Hermione and orders their new-born daughter to be abandoned.

The daughter, Perdita (meaning 'lost'), instead of being cast adrift and killed, is found by a shepherd and eventually returns. Similarly Leontes' wife, whom he had thought dead, and had wrongly accused, comes back to life from a pillar of stone. In the play's resolution, the kings and their children are brought together again, and Perdita and Florizel are married.

### 3 • The Tempest

Quote: *'Our revels now are ended.'*

#### *Dramatis Personae*

1 PROSPERO, the rightful Duke of Milan
2 FERDINAND, son to the King of Naples
3 CALIBAN, a savage and deformed slave
4 TRINCULO, a jester
5 STEPHANO, a drunken butler
6 MIRANDA, daughter to Prospero
7 ARIEL, an airy spirit
8 ALONSO, King of Naples

*The Tempest* is normally considered to be Shakespeare's final play, and again deals with the theme of forgiveness. The play traces the banishment of Prospero, the Duke of Milan, to a distant island, peopled only by mystical fairy spirits, and hobgoblins such as Caliban.

Prospero, using magic powers, releases a spirit, Ariel, who controls a storm, during which King Alonso (the leader of the conspiracy that abandoned Prospero and his daughter Miranda at sea) and his fellow shipmates are shipwrecked.

By magic, Prospero inveigles the usurpers of his dukedom on to the island, cleverly and subtly punishing them. However, when Ferdinand, the son of Alonso, falls in love with Miranda, Alonso gives Prospero back his dukedom and begs for forgiveness. Like the other last plays, *The Tempest* ends with a bitter-sweet reconciliation. Everyone returns to Italy.

# Vocabulary:
## Prefixes, Suffixes
### and Roots

# 13

## Preview

- Prefixes
- Suffixes
- Roots

> The use and manipulation of vocabulary is the one mental skill which,
> above all others, can be most closely correlated with general personal
> success. It is therefore essential, throughout your life, to develop this
> enticing and personally releasing ability.

This may initially seem a daunting task, but happily there is an easy way to spend a little time and gain maximum rewards. In the same way as Meccano and Lego sets use a few basic pieces to create an infinity of shapes and structures, so a vast vocabulary is based upon relatively few prefixes, suffixes and roots.

On the following pages you will find, in order, the major prefixes, suffixes and roots that are liberally sprinkled through every conversation you have, and every article and book you read.

By using SEM$^3$ to remember these key units of vocabulary, you will enhance your memory and your ability to increase your vocabulary and therefore your 'success quotient'. You will also increase your intelligence, because memory and vocabulary skills are two of the main elements in standard intelligence (IQ) Tests.

# Prefixes

(L = Latin; G = Greek; F = French; E = English. Some sources unknown.)

| Prefix | Meaning | Example |
| --- | --- | --- |
| *a-, an-* (G) | without, not | anaerobic |
| *ab-, abs-* (L) | away, from, apart | absent |
| *ad-, ac-, af-* (L) | to, towards | advent, advance |
| *aero-* | air | aeroplane, aeronaut |
| *amb-, ambi-* (G) | both, around | ambiguous |
| *amphi-* (G) | both, around | amphitheatre |
| *ante-* (L) | before | antenatal |
| *anti-* (G) | against | antidote, antitoxic |
| *apo-* (G) | away from | apostasy |
| *arch-* (G) | chief, most important | archbishop, arch-criminal |
| *auto-* (G) | self | automatic, autocrat |
| *be-* | about, make | belittle, beguile, beset |
| *bene-* (L) | well, good | benediction |
| *bi-* (G) | two | biennial, bicycle |
| *by, bye-* (G) | added to | byways, bye-laws |
| *cata-* (G) | down | catalogue, cataract |
| *centi-, cente-* (L) | hundred | centigrade, centenary |
| *circum-* (L) | around | circumference, circumambient |
| *co-, col-, com-, cor-, con-* (L) | together, with | companion, collect, co-operate |
| *contra-* (L) | against, counter | contradict, contraceptive |
| *de-* (F) | down | denude, decentralise |
| *deca-, deci-* (G) | ten | decade, decagon |
| *demi-* (L) | half | demigod |
| *dia-* (G) | through, between | diameter |
| *dis-* (L) | not, opposite to | dislike, disagree |
| *duo-* (G) | two | duologue, duplex |
| *dys-* (G) | ill, hard | dysentery |
| *e-, ex-* | out of | exhale, excavate |
| *ec-* (L) | out of | eccentric |
| *en-, in-, em-, im-* (L, G, F) | into, not | enrage, inability, embolden, emulate, impress |
| *epi-* (G) | upon, at, in addition | epidemic, epidermis |
| *equi-* | equally | equidistant |
| *extra-* (L) | outside, beyond | extramarital |
| *for-, fore-* (E) | before | foresee |
| *hemi-* (G) | half | hemisphere |

| Prefix | Meaning | Example |
|--------|---------|---------|
| *hepta-* (G) | seven | heptagon |
| *hexa-* (G) | six | hexagon, hexateuch |
| *homo-* (L) | same | homonym |
| *hyper-* (G) | above, excessive | hypercritical, hypertrophy |
| *il-* | not | illegal, illogical |
| *in-, im-* (*un-*) (L, G, F) | not | imperfect, inaccessible |
| *inter-* (L) | among, between | interrupt, intermarriage |
| *intra-, intro-* (L) | inside, within | intramural, introvert |
| *iso-* (G) | equal, same | isobaric, isosceles |
| *mal-* (L) | bad, wrong | malfunction, malformed |
| *meta-* (G) | after, beyond | metabolism, metaphysical |
| *mis-* | wrongly | misfit, mislead |
| *mono-* (G) | one, single | monotonous, monocular |
| *multi-* (L) | many | multipurpose, multimillion |
| *non-* | not | nonsense, nonpareil |
| *ob-, oc-, of-,* | in the way of, | obstruct, obstacle, |
| *op-* (L) | resistance | oppose |
| *octa-, octo-* (G) | eight | octahedron, octave |
| *off-* | away, apart | offset |
| *out-* | beyond | outnumber, outstanding |
| *over-* | above | overhear, overcharge |
| *para-* (G) | aside, beyond | parable, paradox |
| *penta-* (G) | five | pentagon, pentateuch |
| *per-* (L) | through | perennial, peradventure |
| *peri-* (G) | around, about | perimeter, pericardium |
| *poly-* (G) | many | polygamy, polytechnic |
| *post-* (L) | after | postscript, postnatal |
| *pre-* (L) | before | prehistoric, pre-war |
| *prime-, primo-* (L) | first, important | primary, Prime Minister |
| *pro-* (L) | in front of, favouring | prologue, pro-British |
| *quadri-* (L) | four | quadrennial, quadrangle |
| *re-* (L) | again, back | reappear, recivilise |
| *retro-* (L) | backward | retrograde, retrospect |
| *se-* | aside | secede |
| *self-* | personalising | self-control, self-taught |
| *semi-* (G) | half | semicircle, semi-detached |
| *sub-* (L) | under | submarine, subterranean |
| *super-* (L) | above, over | superfluous, superior |
| *syl-* | with, together | syllogism |
| *syn-, sym-* (G) | together | sympathy, synchronise |
| *tele-* (G) | far, at or to a distance | telegram, telepathy |
| *ter-* (L) | three times | tercentenary |

| Prefix | Meaning | Example |
|---|---|---|
| *tetra-* (G) | four | tetrahedron, tetralogy |
| *trans-* (L) | across, through | transatlantic, translate |
| *tri-* (L, G) | three | triangle, tripartite |
| *ultra-* (L) | beyond | ultramarine, ultra-violet |
| *un-* (*im-*) (L, G, F) | not | unbroken, unbutton, unable |
| *under-* | below | underfed, underling |
| *uni-* (L) | one | unicellular, uniform |
| *vice-* (L) | in place of | viceroy, vice-president |
| *yester-* (E) | preceding time | yesterday, yesteryear |

## Suffixes

| Suffix | Meaning | Example |
|---|---|---|
| *-able, -ible* (L) | capable of, fit for | durable, comprehensible |
| *-acy* (L, G) | state or quality of | accuracy |
| *-age* (L) | action or state of | breakage |
| *-al, -ial* (L) | relating to | abdominal |
| *-an (-ane, -ian)* (L) | the nature of | Grecian, African |
| *-ance, -ence,* | quality or action of | insurance, corpulence |
| *-ant* (L) | forming adjectives of quality, nouns signifying a personal agent or something producing an effect | defiant, servant |
| *-arium, -orium* (L) | place for | aquarium, auditorium |
| *-ary* (L) | place for, dealing with | seminary, dictionary |
| *-atable* (L) | (*see -able, -ible*) | |
| *-ate* (L) | cause to be, office of | animate, magistrate |
| *-ation, -ition* (L) | action or state of | condition, dilapidation |
| *-cle, -icle* (L) | diminutive | icicle |
| *-dom* (E) | condition or control | kingdom |
| *-en* (E) | small | mitten |
| *-en* (E) | quality | golden, broken |
| *-er* (E) | belonging to | farmer, New Yorker |
| *-ess* (E) | feminine suffix | hostess, waitress |
| *-et, -ette* (L) | small | puppet, marionette |
| *-ferous* (L) | producing | coniferous |
| *-ful* (E) | full of | colourful, beautiful |
| *-fy, -ify* (L) | make | satisfy, fortify |
| *-hood* (E) | state or condition of | boyhood, childhood |
| *-ia* (L) | names of classes, names of places | bacteria, Liberia |

| Suffix | Meaning | Example |
|---|---|---|
| *-ian* (L) | practitioners or inhabitants | musician, Parisian |
| *-ible, -able,* (L) | capable of, fit for | durable, comprehensible |
| *-ic* (G) | relating to | historic |
| *-id(e)* (L) | a quality | acid |
| *-ine* (G, L) | a compound | chlorine |
| *-ion* (L) | condition or action of | persuasion |
| *-ish* (E) | a similarity or relationship | childish, greenish |
| *-ism* (G) | quality or doctrine of | realism, socialism |
| *-ist* (G) | one who practises | chemist, pessimist |
| *-itis* (L) | inflammation of (medical) | bronchitis |
| *-ity, -ety, -ty* (L) | state or quality of | loyalty |
| *-ive* (L) | nature of | creative, receptive |
| *-ize, -ise* (G) | make, practise, act like | modernize, advertise |
| *-lent* (L) | fullness | violent |
| *-less* (E) | lacking | fearless, faceless |
| *-logy* (G) | indicating a branch of knowledge | biology, psychology |
| *-ly* (E) | having the quality of | softly, quickly |
| *-ment* (L) | act or condition of | resentment |
| *-metry, -meter* (G) | measurement | gasometer, geometry |
| *-mony* | resulting condition | testimony |
| *-oid* (G) | resembling | ovoid |
| *-or* (L) | a state or action, a person who, or thing which | error, governor, victor, generator |
| *-osis* | process or condition of | metamorphosis |
| *-ous, -ose* (L) | full of | murderous, anxious, officious, morose |
| *-some* | like | gladsome |
| *-tude* (L) | quality or degree of | altitude, gratitude |
| *-ward* (E) | direction | backward, outward |
| *-y* (E) | condition | difficulty |

# Roots

| Root | Meaning | Example |
|------|---------|---------|
| *aer* | air | aerate, aeroplane |
| *am* (from *amare*) | love | amorous, amateur, amiable |
| *ann* (from *annus*) | year | annual, anniversary |
| *aud* (from *audire*) | hear | auditorium, audit |
| *bio* | life | biography |
| *cap* (from *capire*) | take | captive |
| *cap* (from *caput*) | head | capital, per capita, decapitate |
| *chron* | time | chronology, chronic |
| *cor* | heart | cordial |
| *corp* | body | corporation |
| *de* | god | deify, deity |
| *dic, dict* | say, speak | dictate |
| *duc* (from *ducere*) | lead | aqueduct, duke, ductile |
| *ego* | I | egotism |
| *equi* | equal | equidistant |
| *fac, fic* (from *facere*) | make, do | manufacture, efficient |
| *frat* (from *frater*) | brother | fraternity |
| *geo* | earth | geology |
| *graph* | write | calligraphy, graphology, telegraph |
| *loc* (from *locus*) | place | location, local |
| *loqu, loc* (from *loqui*) | speak | eloquence, circumlocution |
| *luc* (from *lux*) | light | elucidate |
| *man* (from *manus*) | hand | manuscript, manipulate |
| *mit, miss* (from *mittere*) | send | admit, permission |
| *mort* (from *mors*) | death | immortal |
| *omni* | all | omnipotent, omnibus |
| *pat* (from *pater*) | father | paternal |
| *path* | suffering, feeling | sympathy, pathology |
| *ped* (from *pes*) | foot | impede, millepede, pedal |
| *phobia, phobe* | fear | hydrophobe, xenophobia |
| *photo* | light | photography |
| *pneum* | air, breath, spirit | pneumonla |
| *pos, posit* | place | deposit, position |
| *pot, poss, poten* (from *ponerte*) | be able | potential, possible |

| Root | Meaning | Example |
|------|---------|---------|
| *quaerere* | question, seek | inquiry, query |
| *rog* (from *rogare*) | ask | interrogate |
| *scrib, scrip* (from *scribere*) | write | scribble, script, inscribe |
| *sent, sens* (from *sentire*) | feel | sensitive, sentient |
| *sol* | alone | soloist, isolate |
| *soph* | wise | philosopher |
| *spect* (from s*picere*) | look | introspective, inspect |
| *spir* (from *spirare*) | breathe | inspiration |
| *ten* (from *tendere*) | stretch | extend, tense |
| *ten* (from *tenere*) | hold | tenant |
| *therm* (from *thermos*) | warm | thermometer |
| *utilis* | useful | utility |
| *ven, vent* (from *venire*) | come, arrive | advent, convenient |
| *vert, vers* (from *vertere*) | turn | revert, adverse |
| *vid, vis* (from *videre*) | see | supervisor, vision, provident |

# Languages 14

**Preview**

- Italian
- French
- German
- Spanish
- Russian
- Chinese
- Japanese

Fifty per cent of each spoken language is composed of 100 basic key words. For this reason *Master Your Memory* includes the hundred basic words from seven of the world's most common languages.

Applying SEM$^3$ to languages, you simply mark off one of the thousand-cross matrices, say 5000 to 5999, and apply the Memory Principles as before.

For example, let's say you were going to visit Italy, and wished to learn the first 100 words of the Italian vocabulary. If you were using the Sensation 5000 Memory Matrix, and were wanting to remember the eleventh word in the list, 'grande', which means 'big', you would take the Key Memory Image 5011, your father swimming in an Italian sea or lake. You would feel the sensations that your father feels as he swims, and envisage him with a *BIG* smile on his face because the weather is very hot, making it a *GRAND DAY* for a swim!

Memorising vocabulary in this way not only helps you memorise the words but also helps you use imagery and sensation, which are major elements in any successful language learning.

# Italian

| | English | Italian | Italian Pronunciation |
|---|---|---|---|
| 1 | A, an | Un, una | Oon, oona |
| 2 | After | Dietro | Dee-ay'troh |
| 3 | Again | Di nuovo | Dee-noo-oh'voh |
| 4 | All | Tutto | Toot'toh |
| 5 | Almost | Quasi | Kwah'zee |
| 6 | Also | Anche | Ahng'keh |
| 7 | Always | Sempre | Sem'preh |
| 8 | And | E | Ay |
| 9 | Because | Perche | Pehr'kay |
| 10 | Before | Davanti | Dah-vahn'tee |
| 11 | Big | Grande | Grahn'deh |
| 12 | But | Ma | Mah |
| 13 | Can (I can) | Io posso | Ee'oh poss-oh |
| 14 | Come (I come) | Io vengo | Ee'oh ven'go |
| 15 | Either/or | 0/o | Oh/oh |
| 16 | Find (I find) | Io trovo | Ee'oh troh-voh |
| 17 | First | Primo | Pree-moh |
| 18 | For | Per | Pehr |
| 19 | Friend | Amico | Am-ee'coh |
| 20 | From | Da | Dah |
| 21 | Go (I go) | Io vado | Ee'oh vah'doh |
| 22 | Good | Buono | Boo-oh'noh |
| 23 | Goodbye | Arrivederci | Ahr-ree'veh-dehr'chee |
| 24 | Happy | Felice | Fe'lee'cheh |
| 25 | Have (I have) | Io ho | Ee'oh oh |
| 26 | He | Lui | Loo'ee |
| 27 | Hello | Ciao | Chow |
| 28 | Here | Qui | Kwee |
| 29 | How | Come | Koh'meh |
| 30 | I | Io | Ee'oh |
| 31 | I am | Sono | Soh'noh |
| 32 | If | Se | Seh |
| 33 | In | In | Een |
| 34 | Know (I know) | Io conosco | Ee'oh koh-noh-sco |
| 35 | Last | Scorso | Skorr'soh |
| 36 | Like (I like) | Mi piace | Mee pee-ah'cheh |
| 37 | Little | Poco | Poh'koh |
| 38 | Love (I love) | Io amo | Eeh'oh am'oh |
| 39 | Make (I make) | Io faccio | Ee'oh fa'choh |
| 40 | Many | Molti | Moll-tee |
| 41 | Me | Mi | Mee |
| 42 | More | Più | Pee'oo |

| | English | Italian | Italian Pronunciation |
|---|---|---|---|
| 43 | Most | Il più | Eel pee'oo |
| 44 | Much | Molto | Moll'toh |
| 45 | My | Mio | Mee'oh |
| 46 | New | Nuovo | Noo-oh'voh |
| 47 | No | No | Noh |
| 48 | Not | Non | Nonn |
| 49 | Now | Ora | Oh'rah |
| 50 | Of | Di | Dee |
| 51 | Often | Spesso | Spess'soh |
| 52 | On | Su | Soo |
| 53 | One | Uno | Oon'oh |
| 54 | Only | Solo | Soh'loh |
| 55 | Or | O | Oh |
| 56 | Other | Altro | Ahl'troh |
| 57 | Our | Il nostro | Eel noss'troh |
| 58 | Out | Fuori | Foo-oh'ree |
| 59 | Over | Attraverso | Aht'trah-vehr'soh |
| 60 | People | Gente | Jen'teh |
| 61 | Place | Luogo | Loo-oh'goh |
| 62 | Please | Per favore | Pehr fah-voh'reh |
| 63 | Same | Medesimo | Meh-day'zeemoh |
| 64 | See (I see) | Io vedo | Eeh'oh vay-doh |
| 65 | She | Lei | Lay'ee |
| 66 | So | Così | Koh'zee |
| 67 | Some | Qualche | Kwahl'keh |
| 68 | Sometimes | Talvolta | Tahl-voll'tah |
| 69 | Still | Ancora | Ahng'koh-rah |
| 70 | Such | Tale | Tah'lay |
| 71 | Tell (I tell) | Io racconto | Ee'oh rak-kon'toh |
| 72 | Thank you | Grazie | Grah'tsee-eh |
| 73 | That | Quello | Kwell'loh |
| 74 | The | Il, la | Eel, lah |
| 75 | Their | Il loro, la loro | Eel loh'roh, lah loh'roh |
| 76 | Them | Li, le, loro | Lee, lay, loh'roh |
| 77 | Then | Allora | Ahl-loh'rah |
| 78 | There is, there are | C'e, ci sono | Cheh, chee soh-noh |
| 79 | They | Loro | Loh'roh |
| 80 | Thing | Cosa | Koh'sah |
| 81 | Think (I think) | Io penso | Eeh'oh pen-soh |
| 82 | This | Questo | Kwess'toh |
| 83 | Time | Ora | Oh'rah |
| 84 | To | Per | Pehr |
| 85 | Under | Più basso | Pee-oo bahs'soh |
| 86 | Up | Su per | Soo pehr |

| | English | Italian | Italian Pronunciation |
|---|---|---|---|
| 87 | Us | Noi | Noh'ee |
| 88 | Use (I use) | Io uso | Eeh'oh oo-zoh |
| 89 | Very | Molto | Moll'toh |
| 90 | We | Noi | Noy |
| 91 | What | Come | Koh'may |
| 92 | When | Quando | Kwahn'doh |
| 93 | Where | Dove | Doh'veh |
| 94 | Which | Quale | Kwah'leh |
| 95 | Who | Chi | Kee |
| 96 | Why | Perché | Pehr-keh |
| 97 | With | Con | Kon |
| 98 | Yes | Si | See |
| 99 | You | Tu | Too |
| 100 | Your | Il suo, la sua | Eel soo'oh, lah soo'ah |

# French

* 'Je' is pronounced like the 'zh' sound in 'pleasure' or 'beige'. Where (n) is in brackets, it is pronounced nasally.

| | English | French | French Pronunciation |
|---|---|---|---|
| 1 | A, an | Un, une | Er(n), oon |
| 2 | After | Après | A'pray |
| 3 | Again | Encore | O(n)'kor |
| 4 | All | Tout, toute | Too, toot |
| 5 | Almost | Presque | Press'ke |
| 6 | Also | Aussi | Oh'see |
| 7 | Always | Toujours | Too'zhure |
| 8 | And | Et | Ay |
| 9 | Because | Parce que | Pah'ske |
| 10 | Before | Avant | A'vo(n) |
| 11 | Big | Grand, Grande | Gro(n), Gro(n)d |
| 12 | But | Mais | May |
| 13 | Can (I can) | Je peux | *Je pe |
| 14 | Come (I come) | Je viens | *Je vee'a(n) |
| 15 | Either/or | Ou/ou | Ooh/ooh |
| 16 | Find (I find) | Je trouve | *Je troov |
| 17 | First | Premier | Preh'mee'ay |
| 18 | For | Pour | Poor |
| 19 | Friend | Ami, Amie | Am'ee, Am'ee |
| 20 | From | De | De |
| 21 | Go (I go) | Je vais | *Je vay |
| 22 | Good | Bien | Bee'a(n) |
| 23 | Goodbye | Au revoir | O-re'vwa |

| | English | French | French Pronunciation |
|---|---|---|---|
| 24 | Happy | Content, Contente | Ko(n)'to(n), Ko(n)'tont |
| 25 | Have (I have) | J'ai | *Jay |
| 26 | He | Il | Eel |
| 27 | Hello | Bonjour | Bo(n)'zhure |
| 28 | Here | Ici | Ee'see |
| 29 | How | Comment | Kom'o(n) |
| 30 | I | Je | *Je |
| 31 | I am | Je suis | *Je swee |
| 32 | If | Si | See |
| 33 | In | Dans | Do(n) |
| 34 | Know (I know) | Je sais | *Je say |
| 35 | Last | Dernier | Dair'nee'ay |
| 36 | Like (I like) | J'aime | *Jem |
| 37 | Little | Petit, Petite | Pe'tee, Pe'teet |
| 38 | Love (I love) | J'aime | *Jem |
| 39 | Make (I make) | Je fais | *Je fay |
| 40 | Many | Beaucoup | Bo'ku |
| 41 | Me | Moi | Mwa |
| 42 | More | Plus | Ploo |
| 43 | Most | La plupart | La ploo'par |
| 44 | Much | Beaucoup | Bo'ku |
| 45 | My | Mon, Ma | Mo(n), Ma |
| 46 | New | Nouveau, nouvelle | Nu'vo, nu'vel |
| 47 | No | Non | No(n) |
| 48 | Not | Ne pas | Ne pah |
| 49 | Now | Maintenant | Ma(n)'te'no(n) |
| 50 | Of | De | De |
| 51 | Often | Souvent | Soo'von(n) |
| 52 | On | Sur | S'ure |
| 53 | One | Un, Une | Er(n), Oon |
| 54 | Only | Seulement | Serl'e'mo(n) |
| 55 | Or | Ou | Ooh |
| 56 | Other | Autre | Oh'tr |
| 57 | Our | Notre | No'tr |
| 58 | Out | Dehors | De'or |
| 59 | Over | Pardessus | Par'de'soo |
| 60 | People | Les gens | Lay *jo(n) |
| 61 | Place | Place | Plas |
| 62 | Please | S'il vous plaît | Seel voo play |
| 63 | Same | Même | Memm |
| 64 | See (I see) | Je vois | *Je vwa |
| 65 | She | Elle | El |
| 66 | So | Donc | Do(n)k |

| | English | French | French Pronunciation |
|---|---|---|---|
| 67 | Some | Quelque | Kel'ke |
| 68 | Sometimes | Quelquefois | Kel'ke fwa |
| 69 | Still | Encore | O(n)'kor |
| 70 | Such | Tel | Tell |
| 71 | Tell (I tell) | Je dis | *Je dee |
| 72 | Thank you | Merci | Mair'see |
| 73 | That | Que | Ke |
| 74 | The | Le, la | Le, lah |
| 75 | Their | Leur | Ler |
| 76 | Them | Les | Lay |
| 77 | Then | Alors | Ah-loh're |
| 78 | There is, there are | Il y a | Eel ee ar |
| 79 | They | Ils, elles | Eel, ell |
| 80 | Thing | Chose | Sh'ohs |
| 81 | Think (I think) | Je pense | *Je po(n)se |
| 82 | This | Ce, cette | Se, set |
| 83 | Time | Temps | To(n) |
| 84 | To | A | Ah |
| 85 | Under | Sous | Soo |
| 86 | Up | En haut | On'oh |
| 87 | Us | Nous | Noo |
| 88 | Use (I use) | J'utilise | *Joo'tee'lees |
| 89 | Very | Très | Tray |
| 90 | We | Nous | Noo |
| 91 | What | Que | Ke |
| 92 | When | Quand | Ko(n) |
| 93 | Where | Où | Ooh |
| 94 | Which | Quel, quelle | Kel, kel |
| 95 | Who | Qui | Kee |
| 96 | Why | Pourquoi | Poor kwah |
| 97 | With | Avec | A'vek |
| 98 | Yes | Oui | Wee |
| 99 | You | Tu, vous | Too, voo |
| 100 | Your | Ton, tes, votre, vos | To(n), tay, vot're, voh |

# German

Pronunciation: 'w' is pronounced as 'v', and v' is pronounced as 'f', 'g' as in 'goat', 'k' as in 'loch', 'ü' as in 'soon' and 'u' as in 'foot'.

| | English | German | German Pronunciation |
|---|---|---|---|
| 1 | A, an | Ein, eine | Ine, i-ne |
| 2 | After | Nach | Nahk |
| 3 | Again | Wieder | Vee-dair |

| | English | German | German Pronunciation |
|---|---|---|---|
| 4 | All | Alle | Ul-le |
| 5 | Almost | Beinahe | By-nah |
| 6 | Also | Auch | Owk |
| 7 | Always | Immer | Im'me |
| 8 | And | Und | Oont |
| 9 | Because | Weil | Vile |
| 10 | Before | Vorne | Fawrne |
| 11 | Big | Gross | Grohs |
| 12 | But | Aber | Ar'be |
| 13 | Can (I can) | Ich kann | Ik kan |
| 14 | Come (I come) | Ich komme | Ik komm'e |
| 15 | Either/or | Entweder/oder | Ent'vay'der/oh'der |
| 16 | Find (I find) | Ich finde | Ik fin'de |
| 17 | First | Erst | Air'st |
| 18 | For | Für | Fewr |
| 19 | Friend | Freund | Froynt |
| 20 | From | Von | Fon |
| 21 | Go (I go) | Ich gehe | Ik gay'e |
| 22 | Good | Gut | Goot |
| 23 | Goodbye | Auf wiedersehen | Owf' vee'dair-zay-en |
| 24 | Happy | Glücklich | Glewk'lik |
| 25 | Have (I have) | Ich habe | Ik hah'be |
| 26 | He | Er | Air |
| 27 | Hello | Guten tag | Goot'en tahg |
| 28 | Here | Hier | Heer |
| 29 | How | Wie | Vee |
| 30 | I | Ich | Ik |
| 31 | I am | Ich bin | Ik bin |
| 32 | If | Wenn | Ven |
| 33 | In | In | In |
| 34 | Know (I know) | Ich weiss | Ik vice |
| 35 | Last | Letzt | Let's't |
| 36 | Like (I like) | Ich mag | Ik mahg |
| 37 | Little | Klein | Kline |
| 38 | Love (I love) | Ich liebe | Ik lee'be |
| 39 | Make (I make) | Ich mache | Ik mu'ke |
| 40 | Many | Viel | Feel |
| 41 | Me | Mich | Mik |
| 42 | More | Mehr | M'air |
| 43 | Most | Die meisten | Dee my'sten |
| 44 | Much | Viel | Feel |
| 45 | My | Mein | Mine |
| 46 | New | Neu | Noy |
| 47 | No | Nein | Nine |

| | **English** | **German** | **German Pronunciation** |
|---|---|---|---|
| 48 | Not | Nicht | Nikt |
| 49 | Now | Jetzt | Yet's't |
| 50 | Of | Von | Fon |
| 51 | Often | Oft | Off't |
| 52 | On | Auf | Owf |
| 53 | One | Ein | Ine |
| 54 | Only | Nur | Newr |
| 55 | Or | Oder | O'de |
| 56 | Other | Andere | Un'de're |
| 57 | Our | Unser | Oon'sair |
| 58 | Out | Aus | Ows |
| 59 | Over | Über | Oo'bair |
| 60 | People | Leute | Loy'te |
| 61 | Place | Platz | Plahts |
| 62 | Please | Bitte | Bitter |
| 63 | Same | Derselbe, dieselbe, dasselbe | Dair'sel'be dee'sel'be duss'sel'be |
| 64 | See (I see) | Ich sehe | Ik say'e |
| 65 | She | Sie | Zee |
| 66 | So | So | Zoh |
| 67 | Some | Etwas | Et'vahss |
| 68 | Sometimes | Manchmal | Monk'mahl |
| 69 | Still | Noch | Nok |
| 70 | Such | Solch | Solk |
| 71 | Tell (I tell) | Ich erzähle | Ik air'zay'le |
| 72 | Thank you | Danke | Dahnn'ke |
| 73 | That | Das, dass | Duss |
| 74 | The | Der, die, das | Dair, dee, duss |
| 75 | Their | Ihr | Eer |
| 76 | Them | Sie | Zee |
| 77 | Then | Dann | Dahnn |
| 78 | There is, There are | Es gibt | Ess gib't |
| 79 | They | Sie | Zee |
| 80 | Thing | Die Sache | Dee sah'ke |
| 81 | Think (I think) | Ich denke | Ik den'ke |
| 82 | This | Diese | Dee'ze |
| 83 | Time | Zeit | Tsite |
| 84 | To | Nach | Nahk |
| 85 | Under | Unter | Oon'te |
| 86 | Up | Auf | Ow'f |
| 87 | Us | Uns | Oon's |
| 88 | Use (I use) | Ich gebrauche | Ik gay'brow'ke |
| 89 | Very | Sehr | Zare |
| 90 | We | Wir | Veer |

| 91 | What | Was | Vahss |
| 92 | When | Wann | Vun |
| 93 | Where | Wo | Voh |
| 94 | Which | Welche | Vel'ke |
| 95 | Who | Wer | Vair |
| 96 | Why | Warum | Var'oom |
| 97 | With | Mit | Mitt |
| 98 | Yes | Ja | Yah |
| 99 | You | Du, sie | Doo, zee |
| 100 | Your | Ihr, eure | Ear, oy'er |

## Spanish

| | **English** | **Spanish** | **Spanish Pronunciation** |
| --- | --- | --- | --- |
| 1 | A, an | Un, uno, una | Oon, oo'no, oo'na |
| 2 | After | Después | Days-pues |
| 3 | Again | De nuevo | Day nway'vo |
| 4 | All | Todo | To'do |
| 5 | Almost | Casi | Ka'see |
| 6 | Also | También | Tam-byayn |
| 7 | Always | Siempre | Syem'pray |
| 8 | And | Y | Ee |
| 9 | Because | Porque | Por'kay |
| 10 | Before | Ante | An'tay |
| 11 | Big | Grande | Gran'day |
| 12 | But | Pero | Pay'ro |
| 13 | Can (I can) | Puedo | Pway'do |
| 14 | Come (I come) | Vengo | Ven'go |
| 15 | Either/or | 0/o | Oh/oh |
| 16 | Find (I find) | Encuentro | En-kwen'tro |
| 17 | First | Primero | Pree-may'ro |
| 18 | For | Por | Por |
| 19 | Friend | Amigo | Ah'mee'go |
| 20 | From | De | Day |
| 21 | Go (I go) | Voy | Voy |
| 22 | Good | Bueno | Bway'no |
| 23 | Goodbye | Adiós | Ah'dyos |
| 24 | Happy | Contento | Con'ten'to |
| 25 | Have (I have) | Tengo | Tayn-go |
| 26 | He | El | Ell |
| 27 | Hello | Buenas días | Bway'nas dee'as |
| 28 | Here | Aquí | Ah-kee |
| 29 | How | Cómo | Ko'mo |
| 30 | I | Yo | Yo |
| 31 | I am | Soy | Soy |
| 32 | If | Si | See |

| | English | Spanish | Spanish Pronunciation |
|---|---|---|---|
| 33 | In | En | En |
| 34 | Know (I know) | Sabo | Sa-bo |
| 35 | Last | Último | Ool'tee-mo |
| 36 | Like (I like) | Gusto | Goos-to |
| 37 | Little | Poco | Po'ko |
| 38 | Love (I love) | Amo | Ah'mo |
| 39 | Make (I make) | Hago | Ar'go |
| 40 | Many | Muchos | Moo'chos |
| 41 | Me | Me | May |
| 42 | More | Más | MaHs |
| 43 | Most | Lo más | Lo maHs |
| 44 | Much | Mucho | Moo'cho |
| 45 | My | Mi | Mee |
| 46 | New | Nuevo | Nway'vo |
| 47 | No | No | No |
| 48 | Not | No | No |
| 49 | Now | Ahora | A-o'ra |
| 50 | Of | De | Day |
| 51 | Often | Frecuentemente | Fray-kwen'tay' men'tay |
| 52 | On | Sobre | So'bray |
| 53 | One | Uno | Oo'no |
| 54 | Only | Solo | So'lo |
| 55 | Or | O | O |
| 56 | Other | Otro | O'tro |
| 57 | Our | Nuestro | Nway'stro |
| 58 | Out | Fuera | Fway'ra |
| 59 | Over | Sobre | So'bray |
| 60 | People | Gente | Hen'tay |
| 61 | Place | Lugar | Loo-gar |
| 62 | Please | Por favor | Por fa'vor |
| 63 | Same | Mismo | Mees'mo |
| 64 | See (I see) | Veo | Vay'o |
| 65 | She | Ella | El'lya |
| 66 | So | Así | Ah-see |
| 67 | Some | Algun | Al-goon |
| 68 | Sometimes | Algunas veces | Al-goo'nas vaythes |
| 69 | Still | Siempre | Syem'pray |
| 70 | Such | Tal | Tal |
| 71 | Tell (I tell) | Digo | Dee'go |
| 72 | Thank you | Gracias | Gra'thyas |
| 73 | That | Ese | Ay'say |
| 74 | The | El, la, lo | El, lah, loh |
| 75 | Their | Su, sus | Soo, soos |
| 76 | Them | Los, las, les | Los, lahss, lays |

| | English | Spanish | Spanish Pronunciation |
|---|---|---|---|
| 77 | Then | Luego | Lway'go |
| 78 | There is, there are | Hay | Aye |
| 79 | They | Ellos, ellas | Ay'lyos, Ay'lyahss |
| 80 | Thing | Cosa | Ko'sa |
| 81 | Think (I think) | Pienso | Pyayn-so |
| 82 | This | Este, esta | Ays'tay, ays'tah |
| 83 | Time | Tiempo | Tyem'po |
| 84 | To | A | Ah |
| 85 | Under | Debajo | Day-ba'ho |
| 86 | Up | Arriba | Ah-ree'ba |
| 87 | Us | Nos | Nohs |
| 88 | Use (I use) | Uso | 00'so |
| 89 | Very | Muy | Mwee |
| 90 | We | Nosotros | Nohs'ot'rohs |
| 91 | What | Lo que | Lo kay |
| 92 | When | Cuando | Kwan'do |
| 93 | Where | Dónde | Kwan'do |
| 94 | Which | Que | Kay |
| 95 | Who | Quién | Kee'en |
| 96 | Why | Porque | Por'kay |
| 97 | With | Con | Kon |
| 98 | Yes | Sí | See |
| 99 | You | Tu | Too |
| 100 | Your | Suyo | Soo'yo |

# Russian

Pronunciation at the end of the stressed syllable:

| | | | |
|---|---|---|---|
| kh | as in loch | eh as in hair | |
| zh | as in pleasure | o as in dock | |
| a | as in car | oh as in order | |
| e | as in bet | uh as in duck | |
| ooi | a single sound with the emphasis on the 'i' | | |

| | English | Russian | Russian Pronunciation |
|---|---|---|---|
| 1 | A, an | – | – |
| 2 | After | Posle | Poh'slye |
| 3 | Again | Eshche | Yesh-cho' |
| 4 | All | Vse | Fsye |
| 5 | Almost | Pochti | Puhch-tee' |
| 6 | Also | Tozhe | Toh'zhe |
| 7 | Always | Vsegda | Fsyeg-da' |
| 8 | And | I | Ee |
| 9 | Because | Potomu chto | Puh-tuh-moo'shto |
| 10 | Before | Do | Doh |

| | English | Russian | Russian Pronunciation |
|---|---|---|---|
| 11 | Big | Bolshoi | Buhl-shoi |
| 12 | But | No | No |
| 13 | Can (I can) | Ya mogu | Ya muh-goo |
| 14 | Come (I come) | Ya pridu | Yah pree-doo |
| 15 | Either/or | lli/ili | Ee'li/ee'li |
| 16 | Find (I find) | Ya naidu | Ya nuhee-doo |
| 17 | First | Pervyi | Pyehr'vooi |
| 18 | For | Dlya | Dlyah |
| 19 | Friend | Dryg | Droog |
| 20 | From | Ot | Ot |
| 21 | Go (I go) | Ya idu | Ya ee-doo' |
| 22 | Good | Khorosho | Khu-ruh-shoh' |
| 23 | Goodbye | Do svidaniya | Duh-svi-dan'yuh |
| 24 | Happy | Schastlivyi | Schuhst-lee'vooi |
| 25 | Have (I have) | Ya imeyu | Ya eem-yay'yoo |
| 26 | He | On | Ohn |
| 27 | Hello | Sdravstvuite | Zdrafst'vooi-tye |
| 28 | Here | Zdes | Zdyays |
| 29 | How | Kak | Kak |
| 30 | I | Ya | Yah |
| 31 | I am | Ya | Yah |
| 32 | If | Esli | Yasy'lee |
| 33 | In | V | V |
| 34 | Know (I know) | Ya znayu | Yah znaee'yoo |
| 35 | Last | Poslednii | Puh'slyay'dnee |
| 36 | Like (I like) | Mne nravitsya | Mnye nra'vi-tsyuh |
| 37 | Little | Malenkii | Ma'lyen-kee |
| 38 | Love (I love) | Ya lyublyu | Ya lyoob-lyoo' |
| 39 | Make (I make) | Ya delayu | Ya dyehl'yoo |
| 40 | Many | Mnogo | Mnoh'goh |
| 41 | Me | Menya | Men-yah |
| 42 | More | Bolshe | Bol'she |
| 43 | Most | Nai-bolshii | Nai-bol'shee |
| 44 | Much | Mnogo | Mnoh'goh |
| 45 | My | Moi | Mo'ee |
| 46 | New | Novyi | Noh'vooee |
| 47 | No | Net | Nyet |
| 48 | Not | Ne | Nye |
| 49 | Now | Teper | Tye-pyehr' |
| 50 | Of | Iz | Is |
| 51 | Often | Chasto | Chuh'stoh |
| 52 | On | Na | Nah |
| 53 | One | Odin | Uh-deen |
| 54 | Only | Tolko | Tohl'koh |
| 55 | Or | Ili | Ee'li |

| | English | Russian | Russian Pronunciation |
|---|---|---|---|
| 56 | Other | Drugoi | Droo-goy |
| 57 | Our | Nash | Nahsh |
| 58 | Out | Iz | Is |
| 59 | Over | Nad | Nahd |
| 60 | People | Lyudi | Lyoo'dee |
| 61 | Place | Mesto | Myes'tuh |
| 62 | Please | Pozhaluista | Puh-zhahl'stah |
| 63 | Same | Samyi | Sahm'ooee |
| 64 | See (I see) | Ya vizhu | Yah vee'zhoo |
| 65 | She | Ona | Uh-nah |
| 66 | So | Tak | Tuhk |
| 67 | Some | Nekotoryi | Nye'kuh-to-rooi |
| 68 | Sometimes | Inogda | Ee-nuhg-dah |
| 69 | Still | Eschcho | Yesh-choh' |
| 70 | Such | Takoi | Tuh-koy |
| 71 | Tell (I tell) | Ya skazhu | Yaskuh-zhoo' |
| 72 | Thank you | Spasibo | Spuh-see'buh |
| 73 | That | Etot | Eh'tuht |
| 74 | The | – | – |
| 75 | Their | Ikh | Eekh |
| 76 | Them | Ikh | Eekh |
| 77 | Then | Togda | Tuhg-dah |
| 78 | There is, There are | Est | Yest |
| 79 | They | Oni | Uh-nee |
| 80 | Thing | Predmet | Pryed-myet' |
| 81 | Think (I think) | Ya dumayu | Yah doo'mah-yoo |
| 82 | This | Etot | Eh'tuht |
| 83 | Time | Vremya | Vry-ay'myuh |
| 84 | To | Na | Nah |
| 85 | Under | Pod | Pod |
| 86 | Up | Naverkh | Nah-vehrkh |
| 87 | Us | Nas | Nahs |
| 88 | Use (I use) | Ya ispolzuyu | Ya is-pol'zoo-yoo |
| 89 | Very | Ochen | Oh'chen |
| 90 | We | Myi | Mooee |
| 91 | What | Chto | Shtoh |
| 92 | When | Kogda | Kuhg-dah |
| 93 | Where | Gde | Gdye |
| 94 | Which | Kakoi | Kuh-koi' |
| 95 | Who | Kto | Ktoh |
| 96 | Why | Pochemu | Puh-che-moo' |
| 97 | With | S | S |
| 98 | Yes | Da | Dah |
| 99 | You | Vyi | Vooee |
| 100 | Your | Vash | Vahsh |

# Chinese

Pronunciation:

| | | | |
|---|---|---|---|
| ow | as in cow | er | as in her |
| ih | as in high | ir | as in sir |
| g | as an initial is hard | | |

| | English | Chinese | Chinese (Pin Yin) Pronunciation |
|---|---|---|---|
| 1 | A, an | Yi, ge | Ee, ger |
| 2 | After | Guo le | Gwo ler |
| 3 | Again | You | Yoh |
| 4 | All | Dou | Doh |
| 5 | Almost | Cha bu duo | Chah boo dwoh |
| 6 | Also | Hai | High |
| 7 | Always | Yong yuan | Yung yooen |
| 8 | And | He | Her |
| 9 | Because | Yin wei | Yin way |
| 10 | Before | Yi gian | Ee chyen |
| 11 | Big | Da | Dah |
| 12 | But | Ke shi | Ker shir |
| 13 | Can (I can) | Ke yi | Ke ee |
| 14 | Come (I come) | Wo lai | Woh lih |
| 15 | Either/or | Huo zhe | Hwoh je |
| 16 | Find (I find) | Wo zhao dao | Woh jow dao |
| 17 | First | Di yi | Dee ee |
| 18 | For | Wei | Way |
| 19 | Friend | Peng you | Pung yo |
| 20 | From | Cong | Tsong |
| 21 | Go (I go) | Wo qu | Woh chew |
| 22 | Good | Hao | How |
| 23 | Goodbye | Zai jian | Dzih jyen |
| 24 | Happy | Gao xing | Gow sing |
| 25 | Have (I have) | Wo you | Woh yo |
| 26 | He | Ta | Tah |
| 27 | Hello | Ni hao | Nee ow |
| 28 | Here | Zhe li | Jer lee |
| 29 | How | Zen me | Dzen mer |
| 30 | I | Wo | Woh |
| 31 | I am | Wo shi | Woh she |
| 32 | If | Ru guo | Rroo gwoh |
| 33 | In | Li | Lee |
| 34 | Know (I know) | Wo zhi dao | Woh jir dow |
| 35 | Last | Zui hou | Dzway hoh |
| 36 | Like (I like) | Wo xi huan | Woh see hwan |
| 37 | Little | Xiao | Seeow |
| 38 | Love (I love) | Wo ai | Woh ih |

| | English | Chinese | Chinese (Pin Yin) Pronunciation |
|---|---|---|---|
| 39 | Make (I make) | Wo zhi zao | Wo jir dzow |
| 40 | Many | Duo | Dwoh |
| 41 | Me | Wo | Woh |
| 42 | More | Geng duo de | Geung dwor der |
| 43 | Most | Zui duo | Dzway dwoh |
| 44 | Much | Duo | Dwoh |
| 45 | My | Wo de | Woh de |
| 46 | New | Xin | Sin |
| 47 | No | Bu | Boo |
| 48 | Not | Bu shi | Boo shir |
| 49 | Now | Xian zai | See'en tsih |
| 50 | Of | De | De |
| 51 | Often | Jing chang | Jing chung |
| 52 | On | Shang | Shung |
| 53 | One | Yi | Ee |
| 54 | Only | Zhi | Je |
| 55 | Or | Huo zhe | Hwor jer |
| 56 | Other | Bie de | Beeye de |
| 57 | Our | Wo men de | Woh men de |
| 58 | Out | Wai | Wih |
| 59 | Over | Shang | Shung |
| 60 | People | Ren min | Ren min |
| 61 | Place | Di fang | Dee fang |
| 62 | Please | Qing | Ching |
| 63 | Same | Tong | Tung |
| 64 | See (I see) | Wo kan jian | Woh kan jyen |
| 65 | She | Ta | Tah |
| 66 | So | Suo yi | Soowoh ee |
| 67 | Some | Yi xie | Ee sye |
| 68 | Sometimes | You shi huo | Yoh she hwoh |
| 69 | Still | Hai | Hih |
| 70 | Such | Na me | Nah me |
| 71 | Tell (I tell) | Wo gao su | Woh gow soo |
| 72 | Thank you | Xie xie | Sye sye |
| 73 | That | Na ge | Nah ge |
| 74 | The | – | – |
| 75 | Their | Ta men de | Tah men de |
| 76 | Them | Ta men | Tah men |
| 77 | Then | Ran Hou | Rran hoh |
| 78 | There is, There are | You | Yoh |
| 79 | They | Ta men | Tah men |
| 80 | Thing | Dong Xi | Dung see |
| 81 | Think (I think) | Xiang | Seeyang |
| 82 | This | Zhei ge | Jay ge |
| 83 | Time | Shi jian | She jen |

| | English | Chinese | Chinese (Pin Yin) Pronunciation |
|---|---|---|---|
| 84 | To | Dao | Dow |
| 85 | Under | Xia | Seeah |
| 86 | Up | Shang | Shung |
| 87 | Us | Wo men | Woh men |
| 88 | Use (I use) | Wo yong | Woh yoong |
| 89 | Very | Hen | Hen |
| 90 | We | Wo men | Woh men |
| 91 | What | Shen me | Shen mer |
| 92 | When | Shen me shi hou | Shen mer shir ho |
| 93 | Where | Zai nar | Tsih nar |
| 94 | Which | Nei ge | Nay ger |
| 95 | Who | Shei | Shay |
| 96 | Why | Wei shi me | Way shir mer |
| 97 | With | Tong | Tung |
| 98 | Yes | Shi | She |
| 99 | You | Ni | Nee |
| 100 | Your | Ni de | Nee de |

# Japanese

| | English | Japanese | Japanese Pronunciation |
|---|---|---|---|
| 1 | A, an | Hitotsu no | Hee-toh-tsoo noh |
| 2 | After | Atode | Ah-toh-deh |
| 3 | Again | Mata | Mah-tah |
| 4 | All | Minna | Meen-nah |
| 5 | Almost | Hotondo | Hoh-tohn-doh |
| 6 | Also | Mata | Mah-tah |
| 7 | Always | Itsumo | Ee-tsoo-moh |
| 8 | And | Soshite | Soh-shee-teh |
| 9 | Because | Node | Noh-deh |
| 10 | Before | Mae ni | Mah-eh nee |
| 11 | Big | Okii | Oh-kee |
| 12 | But | Keredomo | Keh-reh-doh-moh |
| 13 | Can (I can) | Dekiru | Deh-kee-doo |
| 14 | Come (I come) | Kuru | Koo-doo |
| 15 | Either/or | Ka | Kah |
| 16 | Find (I find) | Mitsukeru | Mee-tsoo-keh-doo |
| 17 | First | Hajime | Hah-jee-meh |
| 18 | For | Tamini | Tah-mee-nee |
| 19 | Friend | Tomodachi | Tomo-dar'chee |
| 20 | From | Kara | Kah-rah |
| 21 | Go (I go) | Ikimasu | Ikki'muss |
| 22 | Good | Ii | Ee |
| 23 | Goodbye | Sayonara | Sah-yoh-nah-rah |

| | English | Japanese | Japanese Pronunciation |
|---|---|---|---|
| 24 | Happy | Shiawase | Shee'a-wah'say |
| 25 | Have (I have) | Motte imasu | Moht-teh ee-mahss |
| 26 | He | Kare | Kah-deh |
| 27 | Hello | Konnichi wa | Kohn-nee-chee wah |
| 28 | Here | Koko | Koh-koh |
| 29 | How | Doshite | Doh'shtey |
| 30 | I | Watashi | Wah-tah-shee |
| 31 | I am | Watashi wa | Wah-tah-shee wah |
| 32 | If | Moshi | Moh-shee |
| 33 | In | Ni | Nee |
| 34 | Know (I know) | Shitte imasu | Sheet-teh ee-mahss |
| 35 | Last | Owari | Oh-wah-dee |
| 36 | Like (I like) | Suki | Soo-kee |
| 37 | Little | Chiisai | Chee-sah-ee |
| 38 | Love (I love) | Sukidesu | Soo'kee-dess'oo |
| 39 | Make (I make) | Shitemasu | Shih'ti-muss'oo |
| 40 | Many | Takusan | Tah-koo-sahn |
| 41 | Me | Watashi ni | Wah-tah-shee nee |
| 42 | More | Motto | Moht-toh |
| 43 | Most | Ichidan | Ee-chee-dahn |
| 44 | Much | Takusan | Tah-koo-sahn |
| 45 | My | Watashi no | Wah-tah-she noh |
| 46 | New | Atarashii | Ah-tah-dah-shee |
| 47 | No | Iie | Ee-eh |
| 48 | Not | Shinai | Shee-nah-ee |
| 49 | Now | Ima | Ee-mah |
| 50 | Of | No | Noh |
| 51 | Often | Tabitabi | Tah-bee-tah-bee |
| 52 | On | Ue | Oo-eh |
| 53 | One | Ichi | Ee-chee |
| 54 | Only | Tatta | Taht-tah |
| 55 | Or | Ka | Kah |
| 56 | Other | Hoka | Hoh-kah |
| 57 | Our | Watatshitachi no | Wah-tah-shee-tah-chee noh |
| 58 | Out | Soto | Soh-toh |
| 59 | Over | Ue | Oo-eh |
| 60 | People | Hitobito | Hee-toh-bee-toh |
| 61 | Place | Tokoro | Toh-koh-doh |
| 62 | Please | Kudasai | Koo-dah-sah-ee |
| 63 | Same | Onaji | Oh-noh-jee |
| 64 | See (I see) | Mimasu | Mee-mahss |
| 65 | She | Kanojo | Kah-noh-joh |
| 66 | So | So | Soh |

| | English | Japanese | Japanese Pronunciation |
|---|---|---|---|
| 67 | Some | Ikuraka | Ee-koo-dah-kah |
| 68 | Sometimes | Tokidoki | Toh-kee-doh-kee |
| 69 | Still | Mada | Mah-dah |
| 70 | Such | Sonna | Sohn-nah |
| 71 | Tell (I tell) | Iiamasu | Ee'muss |
| 72 | Thank you | Arigato | Ah-ree-gah-toh |
| 73 | That | Sono | Soh-noh |
| 74 | The | Sono | Soh-noh |
| 75 | Their | Karera no | Kah-deh-dah noh |
| 76 | Them | Karera no | Kah-deh-dah noh |
| 77 | Then | Dewa | Deh-wah |
| 78 | There is, there are | Soko desu | Soh-koh dess |
| 79 | They | Karera | Kah-deh-dah |
| 80 | Thing | Mono | Moh-noh |
| 81 | Think (I think) | Omou | Oh-moh-oo |
| 82 | This | Kono | Koh-noh |
| 83 | Time | Jikan | Jee-kahn |
| 84 | To | Ni | Nee |
| 85 | Under | Shita | Shee-tah |
| 86 | Up | Ue | Oo-eh |
| 87 | Us | Wareware ni | Wah-deh-wah-deh nee |
| 88 | Use (I use) | Tsukau | Tsoo-kah-oo |
| 89 | Very | Taihen | Tie-hehn |
| 90 | We | Watashitachi | Wah-tah-shee-tah-chee |
| 91 | What | Nani | Nah-nee |
| 92 | When | Itsu | Ee-tsoo |
| 93 | Where | Doko | Doh-koh |
| 94 | Which | Dore | Do're |
| 95 | Who | Donata | Do'nah'ta |
| 96 | Why | Naze | Nah'ze |
| 97 | With | De | Den |
| 98 | Yes | Hai | Hie |
| 99 | You | Anata | Ah-nah-tah |
| 100 | Your | Anata no | Ah-nah-tah noh |

# Countries/ Capitals 15

In a period of less than a year you will have a knowledge of the location
of the countries and capitals of the world, and of the current events
that relate to them, that will rank you, literally and mathematically,
as one in a million!

If you regularly watch or listen to the news, or subscribe to a daily
newspaper, then you will be 'confronted' with the countries and
capitals of the world on an almost daily basis. Despite this regular
'familiarity' with the information, most people can name no more
than ten countries with their appropriate capital, and have very
little idea of where each country is.

The reason for this is once again the negative spiral, in which
the more you know you don't know, the more rapidly your mind
becomes confused with the bombardment of new information,
the less is learnt, and the more even what you *do* know eventually
becomes confused.

By memorising each country and its capital, and by mentally
imagining the country's location with the aid of the maps on pages
159 and 160, you will find that the more you see, hear and read
about the countries and the capitals, the more you will know and
remember.

| | Country | Capital |
|---|---|---|
| 1 | Afghanistan | Kabul |
| 2 | Albania | Tiranë |
| 3 | Algeria | Algiers |
| 4 | Andorra | Andorra la Vella |
| 5 | Angola | Luanda |
| 6 | Antigua & Barbuda | St John's |
| 7 | Argentina | Buenos Aires |
| 8 | Armenia | Yerevan |
| 9 | Australia | Canberra |
| 10 | Austria | Vienna |
| 11 | Azerbaijan | Baku |
| 12 | Bahamas | Nassau |
| 13 | Bahrain | Manama |
| 14 | Bangladesh | Dhaka |
| 15 | Barbados | Bridgetown |
| 16 | Belarus | Minsk |
| 17 | Belgium | Brussels |
| 18 | Belize | Belmopan |
| 19 | Benin | Porto-Novo |
| 20 | Bhutan | Thimphu |
| 21 | Bolivia | Sucre |
| 22 | Bosnia & Herzegovina | Sarajevo |
| 23 | Botswana | Gaborone |
| 24 | Brazil | Brasilia |
| 25 | Brunei | Bandar Seri Begawan |
| 26 | Bulgaria | Sofia |
| 27 | Burkina Faso | Ouagadougou |
| 28 | Burundi | Bujumbura |
| 29 | Cambodia | Phnom Penh |
| 30 | Cameroon | Yaoundé |
| 31 | Canada | Ottawa |
| 32 | Cape Verde | Praia |
| 33 | Central African Republic | Bangui |
| 34 | Chad | N'Djamena |
| 35 | Chile | Santiago |
| 36 | China | Beijing |
| 37 | Colombia | Bogotá |
| 38 | Comoros | Moroni |
| 39 | Congo, Republic of | Brazzaville |
| 40 | Congo, Dem. Republic of | Kinshasa |
| 41 | Costa Rica | San José |
| 42 | Côte d'Ivoire | Yamoussoukro |
| 43 | Croatia | Zagreb |
| 44 | Cuba | Havana |
| 45 | Cyprus | Nicosia |
| 46 | Czech Republic | Prague |
| 47 | Denmark | Copenhagen |
| 48 | Djibouti | Djibouti |
| 49 | Dominica | Roseau |

| | Country | Capital |
|---|---|---|
| 50 | Dominican Republic | Santo Domingo |
| 51 | Ecuador | Quito |
| 52 | Egypt | Cairo |
| 53 | El Salvador | San Salvador |
| 54 | Equatorial Guinea | Malabo |
| 55 | Eritrea | Asmara |
| 56 | Estonia | Tallinn |
| 57 | Ethiopia | Addis Ababa |
| 58 | Falkland Islands | Stanley |
| 59 | Fiji | Suva |
| 60 | Finland | Helsinki |
| 61 | France | Paris |
| 62 | French Guiana | Cayenne |
| 63 | Gabon | Libreville |
| 64 | Gambia | Banjul |
| 65 | Georgia | Tbilisi |
| 66 | Germany | Berlin |
| 67 | Ghana | Accra |
| 68 | Greece | Athens |
| 69 | Grenada | St George's |
| 70 | Guatemala | Guatemala City |
| 71 | Guinea | Conakry |
| 72 | Guinea-Bissau | Bissau |
| 73 | Guyana | Georgetown |
| 74 | Haiti | Port-au-Prince |
| 75 | Holy See | Vatican City |
| 76 | Honduras | Tegucigalpa |
| 77 | Hungary | Budapest |
| 78 | Iceland | Reykjavik |
| 79 | India | New Delhi |
| 80 | Indonesia | Jakarta |
| 81 | Iran | Tehran |
| 82 | Iraq | Baghdad |
| 83 | Ireland | Dublin |
| 84 | Israel | Jerusalem |
| 85 | Italy | Rome |
| 86 | Jamaica | Kingston |
| 87 | Japan | Tokyo |
| 88 | Jordan | Amman |
| 89 | Kazakhstan | Astana |
| 90 | Kenya | Nairobi |
| 91 | Kiribati | Tarawa |
| 92 | Kuwait | Kuwait |
| 93 | Kyrgyzstan | Bishkek |
| 94 | Laos | Vientiane |
| 95 | Latvia | Riga |
| 96 | Lebanon | Beirut |
| 97 | Lesotho | Maseru |

| | Country | Capital |
|---|---|---|
| 98 | Liberia | Monrovia |
| 99 | Libya | Tripoli |
| 100 | Liechtenstein | Vaduz |
| 101 | Lithuania | Vilnius |
| 102 | Luxembourg | Luxembourg |
| 103 | Macedonia, F.Y.R. of | Skopje |
| 104 | Madagascar | Antananarivo |
| 105 | Malawi | Lilongwe |
| 106 | Malaysia | Kuala Lumpur |
| 107 | Maldives | Malé |
| 108 | Mali | Bamako |
| 109 | Malta | Valletta |
| 110 | Marshall Islands | Majuro |
| 111 | Mauritania | Nouakchott |
| 112 | Mauritius | Port Louis |
| 113 | Mexico | Mexico City |
| 114 | Moldova | Chisinau |
| 115 | Monaco | Monaco-Ville |
| 116 | Mongolia | Ulaanbaatar |
| 117 | Morocco | Rabat |
| 118 | Mozambique | Maputo |
| 119 | Myanmar (formerly Burma) | Pyinmana (formerly Rangoon) |
| 120 | Namibia | Windhoek |
| 121 | Nepal | Kathmandu |
| 122 | Netherlands | Amsterdam |
| 123 | New Zealand | Wellington |
| 124 | Nicaragua | Managua |
| 125 | Niger | Niamey |
| 126 | Nigeria | Abuja |
| 127 | North Korea | Pyongyang |
| 128 | Norway | Oslo |
| 129 | Oman | Muscat |
| 130 | Pakistan | Islamabad |
| 131 | Palau | Koror |
| 132 | Panama | Panama City |
| 133 | Papua New Guinea | Port Moresby |
| 134 | Paraguay | Asunción |
| 135 | Peru | Lima |
| 136 | Philippines | Manila |
| 137 | Poland | Warsaw |
| 138 | Portugal | Lisbon |
| 139 | Puerto Rico | San Juan |
| 140 | Qatar | Doha |
| 141 | Romania | Bucharest |
| 142 | Russia | Moscow |
| 143 | Rwanda | Kigali |
| 144 | St Kitts & Nevis | Basseterre |
| 145 | St Lucia | Castries |

| | Country | Capital |
|---|---|---|
| 146 | St Vincent | Kingstown |
| 147 | Samoa | Apia |
| 148 | São Tomé & Príncipe | São Tomé |
| 149 | Saudi Arabia | Riyadh |
| 150 | Senegal | Dakar |
| 151 | Serbia & Montenegro | Belgrade & Podgorica |
| 152 | Seychelles | Victoria |
| 153 | Sierra Leone | Freetown |
| 154 | Singapore | Singapore |
| 155 | Slovakia | Bratislava |
| 156 | Slovenia | Ljubljana |
| 157 | Solomon Islands | Honiara |
| 158 | Somalia | Mogadishu |
| 159 | South Africa | Pretoria |
| 160 | South Korea | Seoul |
| 161 | Spain | Madrid |
| 162 | Sri Lanka | Colombo |
| 163 | Sudan | Khartoum |
| 164 | Suriname | Paramaribo |
| 165 | Swaziland | Mbabane |
| 166 | Sweden | Stockholm |
| 167 | Switzerland | Bern |
| 168 | Syria | Damascus |
| 169 | Taiwan | Taipei |
| 170 | Tajikistan | Dushanbe |
| 171 | Tanzania | Dadoma |
| 172 | Thailand | Bangkok |
| 173 | Togo | Lomé |
| 174 | Tonga | Nuku'alofa |
| 175 | Trinidad & Tobago | Port-of-Spain |
| 176 | Tunisia | Tunis |
| 177 | Turkey | Ankara |
| 178 | Turkmenistan | Ashgabat |
| 179 | Tuvalu | Funafuti |
| 180 | Uganda | Kampala |
| 181 | Ukraine | Kyiv |
| 182 | United Arab Emirates | Abu Dhabi |
| 183 | United Kingdom | London |
| 184 | United States | Washington |
| 185 | Uruguay | Montevideo |
| 186 | Uzbekistan | Tashkent |
| 187 | Vanuatu | Port-Vila |
| 188 | Venezuela | Caracas |
| 189 | Vietnam | Hanoi |
| 190 | Western Sahara | El Aaiún |
| 191 | Yemen | Sana'a |
| 192 | Zambia | Lusaka |
| 193 | Zimbabwe | Harare |

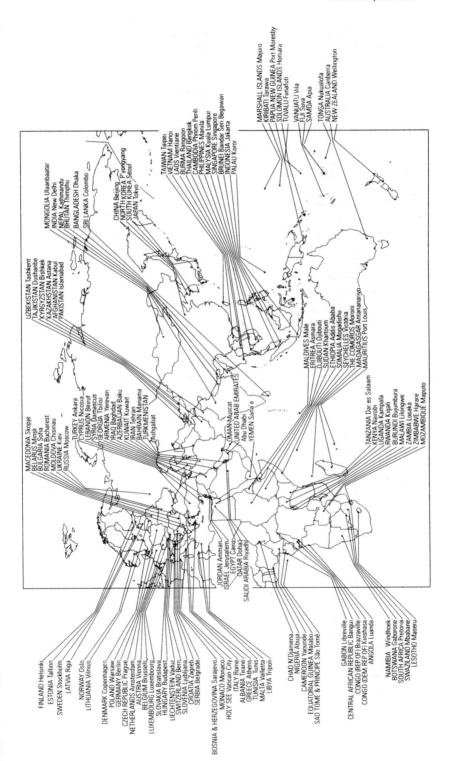

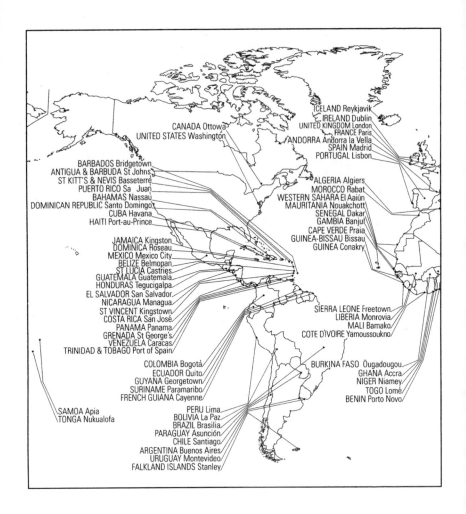

ICELAND Reykjavik
IRELAND Dublin
UNITED KINGDOM London
FRANCE Paris
ANDORRA Andorra la Vella
SPAIN Madrid
PORTUGAL Lisbon

CANADA Ottowa
UNITED STATES Washington

BARBADOS Bridgetown
ANTIGUA & BARBUDA St Johns
ST KITT'S & NEVIS Basseterre
PUERTO RICO Sa    Juan
BAHAMAS Nassau
DOMINICAN REPUBLIC Santo Domingo
CUBA Havana
HAITI Port-au-Prince

ALGERIA Algiers
MOROCCO Rabat
WESTERN SAHARA El Aaiún
MAURITANIA Nouakchott
SENEGAL Dakar
GAMBIA Banjul
CAPE VERDE Praia
GUINEA-BISSAU Bissau
GUINEA Conakry

JAMAICA Kingston
DOMINICA Roseau
MEXICO Mexico City
BELIZE Belmopan
ST LUCIA Castries
GUATEMALA Guatemala
HONDURAS Tegucigalpa
EL SALVADOR San Salvador
NICARAGUA Managua
ST VINCENT Kingstown
COSTA RICA San José
PANAMA Panama
GRENADA St George's
VENEZUELA Caracas
TRINIDAD & TOBAGO Port of Spain

SIERRA LEONE Freetown
LIBERIA Monrovia
MALI Bamako
COTE D'IVOIRE Yamoussoukno

COLOMBIA Bogotà
ECUADOR Quito
GUYANA Georgetown
SURINAME Paramaribo
FRENCH GUIANA Cayenne

BURKINA FASO  Ougadougou
GHANA Accra
NIGER Niamey
TOGO Lomé
BENIN Porto Novo

SAMOA Apia
TONGA Nukualofa

PERU Lima
BOLIVIA La Paz
BRAZIL Brasilia
PARAGUAY Asunción
CHILE Santiago
ARGENTINA Buenos Aires
URUGUAY Montevideo
FALKLAND ISLANDS Stanley

# Kings and Queens of England

## 16

For those who are in any way interested in the history of England, knowledge of the time-location and duration of reign provides an excellent matrix on which to 'hang' other knowledge matrices, including social, literary, religious, musical, artistic and scientific developments.

## Onword

By this stage your skill with SEM$^3$ should have reached such a level that memorising this entire chunk of history (a task considered practically impossible by most history students) will take less than an hour!

| | | From | To |
|---|---|---|---|
| 1 | **William I** | 1066 | 1087 |
| 2 | **William II** | 1087 | 1100 |
| 3 | **Henry I** | 1100 | 1135 |
| 4 | **Stephen** | 1135 | 1154 |
| 5 | **Henry II** | 1154 | 1189 |
| 6 | **Richard I** | 1189 | 1199 |
| 7 | **John** | 1199 | 1216 |
| 8 | **Henry III** | 1216 | 1272 |
| 9 | **Edward I** | 1272 | 1307 |

|    |                                         | From | To   |
|----|-----------------------------------------|------|------|
| 10 | **Edward II**                           | 1307 | 1327 |
| 11 | **Edward III**                          | 1327 | 1377 |
| 12 | **Richard II**                          | 1377 | 1399 |
| 13 | **Henry IV**                            | 1399 | 1413 |
| 14 | **Henry V**                             | 1413 | 1422 |
| 15 | **Henry VI**                            | 1422 | 1461 |
| 16 | **Edward IV**                           | 1461 | 1483 |
| 17 | **Edward V**                            | 1483 | 1483 |
| 18 | **Richard III**                         | 1483 | 1485 |
| 19 | **Henry VII**                           | 1485 | 1509 |
| 20 | **Henry VIII**                          | 1509 | 1547 |
| 21 | **Edward VI**                           | 1547 | 1553 |
| 22 | **Jane**                                | 1553 | 1553 |
| 23 | **Mary I**                              | 1553 | 1558 |
| 24 | **Elizabeth I**                         | 1558 | 1603 |
| 25 | **James I**                             | 1603 | 1625 |
| 26 | **Charles I**                           | 1625 | 1649 |
| 27 | **Oliver Cromwell:** <br> **Lord Protector** | 1653 | 1658 |
| 28 | **Richard Cromwell:** <br> **Lord Protector** | 1658 | 1659 |
| 29 | **Charles II**                          | 1660 | 1685 |
| 30 | **James II**                            | 1685 | 1688 |
| 31 | **William III**                         | 1688 | 1702 |
| 32 | and **Mary II**                         | 1688 | 1694 |
| 33 | **Anne**                                | 1702 | 1714 |
| 34 | **George I**                            | 1714 | 1727 |
| 35 | **George II**                           | 1727 | 1760 |
| 36 | **George III**                          | 1760 | 1820 |
| 37 | **George IV**                           | 1820 | 1830 |
| 38 | **William IV**                          | 1830 | 1837 |
| 39 | **Victoria**                            | 1837 | 1901 |
| 40 | **Edward VII**                          | 1901 | 1910 |
| 41 | **George V**                            | 1910 | 1936 |
| 42 | **Edward VIII**                         | 1936 | 1936 |
| 43 | **George VI**                           | 1936 | 1952 |
| 44 | **Elizabeth II**                        | 1952 |      |

# The Human Body – 17
## Musculature

Memorising your own musculature gives you a more accurate understanding and appreciation of your own extraordinary complexity, allows you to train yourself with more precision and delicacy, to react more appropriately to any injury or medical condition, and to appreciate even more the accomplishments of those who have trained their own musculature to the level of championship performance.

**Brain Bites**

Mental giants such as Michelangelo and Leonardo da Vinci spent years of their lives investigating the body's intricate interconnections and biophysical mechanics.

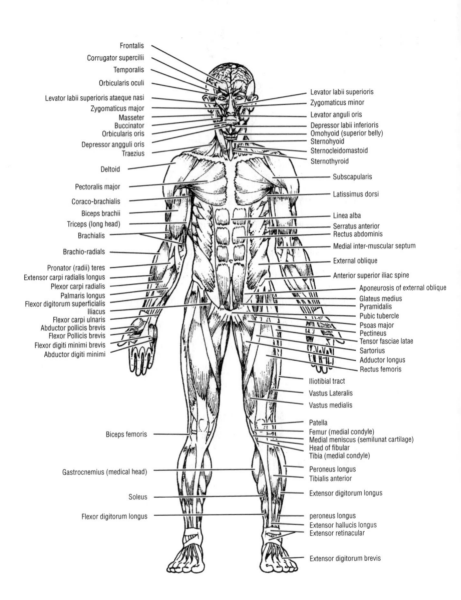

Frontalis
Corrugator supercilii
Temporalis
Orbicularis oculi
Levator labii superioris ataeque nasi
Zygomaticus major
Masseter
Buccinator
Orbicularis oris
Depressor angguli oris
Traezius
Deltoid
Pectoralis major
Coraco-brachialis
Biceps brachii
Triceps (long head)
Brachialis
Brachio-radials
Pronator (radii) teres
Extensor carpi radialis longus
Plexor carpi radialis
Palmaris longus
Flexor digitorum superficialis
Iliacus
Flexor carpi ulnaris
Abductor pollicis brevis
Flexor Pollicis brevis
Flexor digiti minimi brevis
Abductor digiti minimi

Biceps femoris

Gastrocnemius (medical head)

Soleus

Flexor digitorum longus

Levator labii superioris
Zygomaticus minor
Levator anguli oris
Depressor labii inferioris
Omohyoid (superior belly)
Sternohyoid
Sternocleidomastoid
Sternothyroid
Subscapularis
Latissimus dorsi
Linea alba
Serratus anterior
Rectus abdominis
Medial inter-muscular septum
External oblique
Anterior superior iliac spine
Aponeurosis of external oblique
Glateus medius
Pyramidalis
Pubic tubercle
Psoas major
Pectineus
Tensor fasciae latae
Sartorius
Adductor longus
Rectus femoris
Iliotibial tract
Vastus Lateralis
Vastus medialis
Patella
Femur (medial condyle)
Medial meniscus (semilunat cartilage)
Head of fibular
Tibia (medial condyle)
Peroneus longus
Tibialis anterior
Extensor digitorum longus
peroneus longus
Extensor hallucis longus
Extensor retinacular
Extensor digitorum brevis

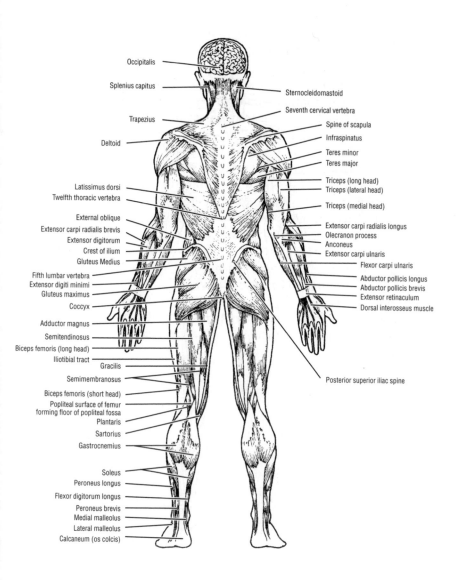

Occipitalis

Splenius capitus

Trapezius

Deltoid

Latissimus dorsi
Twelfth thoracic vertebra

External oblique
Extensor carpi radialis brevis
Extensor digitorum
Crest of ilium
Gluteus Medius

Fifth lumbar vertebra
Extensor digiti minimi
Gluteus maximus
Coccyx

Adductor magnus
Semitendinosus
Biceps femoris (long head)
Iliotibial tract
Gracilis
Semimembranosus

Biceps femoris (short head)
Popliteal surface of femur
forming floor of popliteal fossa
Plantaris
Sartorius
Gastrocnemius

Soleus
Peroneus longus
Flexor digitorum longus
Peroneus brevis
Medial malleolus
Lateral malleolus
Calcaneum (os colcis)

Sternocleidomastoid
Seventh cervical vertebra
Spine of scapula
Infraspinatus
Teres minor
Teres major
Triceps (long head)
Triceps (lateral head)
Triceps (medial head)
Extensor carpi radialis longus
Olecranon process
Anconeus
Extensor carpi ulnaris
Flexor carpi ulnaris
Abductor pollicis longus
Abductor pollicis brevis
Extensor retinaculum
Dorsal interosseus muscle

Posterior superior iliac spine

You would apply SEM$^3$ to the memorisation of the body's musculature (pages 164–5) in the following way: suppose, for example, the first item you want to memorise is the first muscle on the head, i.e. the *Frontalis*. This you will place as number '1' on the Major System – *day*. What does *Frontalis* sound like? How about the 'front of Alice'? You could choose an Alice you know, or, perhaps more preferably, Alice in Wonderland. You might visualise her vividly in a blue dress and white apron with beautiful long, wavy, golden hair. Let's put this information under the Rainbow section of SEM$^3$ and use the colour yellow. Imagine it's the beginning of another wonderful day – a glorious yellow dawn, and over the horizon, instead of the sun, comes Alice! From her *Frontalis* area comes a dazzling yellow light, which suffuses the whole sky, while the rest of Alice gradually rises over the horizon, as the blazing yellow light becomes stronger and stronger. If you have visualised this image well, you will remember where the *Frontalis* area is for the rest of your life.

Let's try one more: *Orbicularis oculi*. This sounds a bit like 'orbit-cular' (an ancient Roman god of the household) -es (the plural of 'lar' is 'lares' -o-culi. Noah's Ark is your number '2'. Paint it a vivid yellow, and on the side of it, painted a darker yellow, is a section of the face that includes the *Orbicularis oculi*. Your special ark, however, is going to go up in *orbit!* In the *cu* of animals are some rather odd-looking characters: twins of the Roman god *lar* (*lares*) and in the middle of them is *oculi*. Easy, isn't it?

# The Elements 18

Our selves, our planet, our solar system and indeed our universe are made up primarily of 105 elements or 'basic working parts'.

Thus the vast majesty of the microcosmos and macrocosmos that surrounds us can, like a language, have its astounding complexity reduced to fundamental operating parts that allow us to understand and learn about it with much greater facility.

Once you have control of these, and the way in which they fit together, your ability to create understanding and inter-relationships and 'structures' within the field becomes limitless.

Using SEM$^3$, you will be able to lay a complete foundation for your growing understanding of the physical, chemical and biological worlds around you – a level of understanding that most people never attain, even after four years of study.

You will also be laying the cornerstones for answering those probing questions that children ask in order to understand the world around them: 'Why does water go hard when it's cold?'; 'Why do things smell and taste different?'; 'Why do sugar and salt taste different although they look the same?'; 'Why do I have to eat?!'

As SEM$^3$ is a Master Matrix that allows you to structure your memory, so the Matrix of the chemical elements is a Master Matrix that allows you to understand the structure and nature of the physical universe.

The names of the various families or groupings of the elements are as follows:

Hydrogen
Noble Gases
Alkali and Alkaline Earth Metals     (abb. Alkaline)
Boron and Carbon Families     (abb. Boron/Carbon)
Nitrogen and Oxygen Families     (abb. Nitrogen/Oxygen)
The Halogens
Early Transition Metals     (abb. Early Trans Metals)
Late Transition Metals     (abb. Late Trans Metals)
The Triads
Rare Earth Metals
Actinide Metals     (abb. Actinide)

| Atomic Number | Elements | Symbol | Atomic Weight | Family |
|---|---|---|---|---|
| 1 | HYDROGEN | H | 1.008 | HYDROGEN |

From hydro and gen, or water-forming; discovered in 1766; third most abundant and lightest element. Hydrogen is almost never found free on earth, but the sun and other stars are almost pure hydrogen. The thermonuclear fusion of hydrogen nuclei lights and heats the universe.

| | | | | |
|---|---|---|---|---|
| 2 | HELIUM | He | 4.0026 | NOBLE GASES |

From helios, or sun; discovered in 1868; almost all the helium in the world comes from natural gas wells in the United States. One well in Arizona produces a gas that is 8% helium. Lighter than air, it is widely used in balloons in place of highly inflammable hydrogen.

| | | | | |
|---|---|---|---|---|
| 3 | LITHIUM | Li | 6.941 | ALKALINE |

From lithos; discovered in 1817; the lightest of the solid elements. Lithium forms a black oxide when exposed to air. It is used in ceramics, alloys, in the H-bomb – and in treating both gout victims and manic-depressives.

| | | | | |
|---|---|---|---|---|
| 4 | BERYLLIUM | Be | 9.012 | ALKALINE |

From the mineral beryl, in which it was found in 1798. This element produces alloys that are extremely elastic, hence its role in making gears, springs and other machine parts. Because of its high melting point – 1285°C – beryllium is used in making rocket nose cones.

| | | | | |
|---|---|---|---|---|
| 5 | BORON | B | 10.811 | BORON/CARBON |

From borax and carbon; discovered 1808. A non-metal, boron is best known in borax (sodium borate) and in boric-acid – the one acid that is good for the eyes. About a million tons of boron are used in industry each year. In agriculture it serves as both a plant food and a weed killer.

| Atomic Number | Elements | Symbol | Atomic Weight | Family |
|---|---|---|---|---|
| 6 | CARBON | C | 12.011 | BORON/CARBON |

From carbo, or charcoal; prehistoric. Carbon, in its endless variety of compounds, is an indispensable source of everyday products, such as nylon and petrol, perfume and plastics, shoe polish, DDT and TNT.

| 7 | NITROGEN | N | 14.007 | NITROGEN/OXYGEN |
|---|---|---|---|---|

From nitron and gen, or nitre-forming; discovered in 1772; a gas making up 78% of the air. Nitrogen can be 'fixed' from the air – compounds include the anaesthetic 'laughing gas', explosives such as TNT, fertilisers and amino acids – the building blocks of protein.

| 8 | OXYGEN | O | 15.999 | NITROGEN/OXYGEN |
|---|---|---|---|---|

From oxys and gen, or acid-forming; discovered in 1774; the most abundant element, making up about half of everything on earth, 21% of the atmosphere by volume and two-thirds of the human body. Breathed in by animals, oxygen is restored to the air by plants.

| 9 | FLUORINE | F | 18.998 | HALOGENS |
|---|---|---|---|---|

From fluor, or flow; discovered in 1771. Fluorine is the most reactive of the non-metals; only a few of the inert gases resist it. It corrodes platinum, a material that withstands most other chemicals. In a stream of fluorine gas, wood and rubber burst into flame – and even asbestos glows.

| 10 | NEON | Ne | 20.183 | NOBLE GASES |
|---|---|---|---|---|

From neos, or new; discovered 1898. The best known of the inert gases, it is chiefly used in advertising. The ubiquitous 'neon sign' is a glass vacuum tube containing a minute amount of neon gas; when an electric current is passed through, the tube gives off a bright orange-red light.

| 11 | SODIUM | Na | 22.990 | ALKALINE |
|---|---|---|---|---|

From soda; symbol from its Latin name Natrium; discovered 1807; sixth most abundant element. Metallic sodium is too violent for most everyday uses and is generally stored in paraffin. But its useful compounds include table salt, baking soda, borax and lye.

| 12 | MAGNESIUM | Mg | 24.3 | ALKALINE |
|---|---|---|---|---|

From Magnesia, an ancient city in Asia Minor; discovered 1775; eighth most abundant element; burns as a powder or foil in firecrackers, bombs and flash bulbs. It has one odd biological effect: a deficiency in man can have the same effect as alcoholism, delirium tremens.

| 13 | ALUMINIUM | Al | 26.982 | BORON/CARBON |
|---|---|---|---|---|

From alumen, or alum; discovered 1827; the most abundant metal and third most abundant element, its uses range from toothpaste tubes to aeroplane wings. Early samples cost £230 per pound; over a million tons are produced yearly in the US for as little as 30 pence per pound.

| Atomic Number | Elements | Symbol | Atomic Weight | Family |
|---|---|---|---|---|
| 14 | SILICON | Si | 28.086 | BORON/CARBON |

From silex, or flint; discovered 1823; the second most abundant element – making up one-quarter of the earth's crust. Sand, largely silicon dioxide, goes into making glass and cement. Pure silicon is used in micro-electronic devices such as solar batteries to power satellite instruments.

| | | | | |
|---|---|---|---|---|
| 15 | PHOSPHORUS | P | 30.974 | NITROGEN/OXYGEN |

From phosphoros, or light bearer; discovered 1669; occurs in three major forms – white, red and rarely black. The white is so unstable that it yellows then reddens in light, glows in the dark – hence 'phosphorescence'. Phosphates are ingredients of detergents.

| | | | | |
|---|---|---|---|---|
| 16 | SULPHUR | S | 32.064 | NITROGEN/OXYGEN |

From sulphur (or brimstone, its biblical name); recognised since ancient times. Used in all branches of modern industry, it is found in matches, insecticides and rubber tyres. Nearly 200 pounds of sulphuric acid per capita are produced in the US each year.

| | | | | |
|---|---|---|---|---|
| 17 | CHLORINE | Cl | 35.453 | HALOGENS |

From chloros, or greenish-yellow; discovered 1774. Combining with almost as many elements as fluorine, chlorine is less corrosive but strong enough to be used as a bleach, a disinfectant and a poison gas. Pure chlorine is commonly prepared from ordinary salt.

| | | | | |
|---|---|---|---|---|
| 18 | ARGON | Ar | 39.948 | NOBLE GASES |

From argon, or inactive; discovered 1894. The most abundant of noble gases, argon makes up 0.934% of the air. Its industrial forte is in welding; it provides an inert atmosphere in which welded metals will not burn. It is also the gas that fills ordinary incandescent light bulbs.

| | | | | |
|---|---|---|---|---|
| 19 | POTASSIUM | K | 39.1 | ALKALINE |

From potash, an impure form of potassium carbonate known to the ancients; symbol K from its Latin name kalium; discovered 1807. Seventh most abundant element in the earth's crust. Its radioactivity, though mild, may be one natural cause of genetic mutation in man.

| | | | | |
|---|---|---|---|---|
| 20 | CALCIUM | Ca | 40.08 | ALKALINE |

From calx, or lime – an oxide of calcium; discovered 1808; fifth most abundant element in the earth's crust. Its presence in our bodies is essential. Normal quota in an adult is about 2 pounds, mostly in the teeth and bones. Calcium also plays a role in regulating the heartbeat.

| | | | | |
|---|---|---|---|---|
| 21 | SCANDIUM | SC | 44.956 | EARLY TRANS METALS |

From Scandinavia; discovered 1879. Although no practical uses have yet been found for this metal, its potential is great because it is almost as light as aluminium and has a much higher melting point. A pound of scandium produced in 1960 was the first such quantity

| Atomic Number | Elements | Symbol | Atomic Weight | Family |
|---|---|---|---|---|
| 22 | TITANIUM | Ti | 47.9 | EARLY TRANS METALS |

From Titans, the supermen of Greek myth; discovered in 1791. Although it is the ninth most abundant element, titanium has only recently begun to serve man. Its white dioxide goes into bright paints. The metal itself is used in constructing supersonic aircraft such as Concorde.

| | | | | |
|---|---|---|---|---|
| 23 | VANADIUM | V | 50.942 | EARLY TRANS METALS |

From Vanadis, a Scandinavian goddess; discovered 1830. Added to steel, vanadium produces one of the toughest alloys for armour plate, axles, piston rods and crankshafts. Less than 1% of vanadium and a little chromium makes steel shock- and vibration-resistant.

| | | | | |
|---|---|---|---|---|
| 24 | CHROMIUM | Cr | 51.996 | EARLY TRANS METALS |

From chroma, or colour; discovered 1797. A very bright silvery metal, it forms compounds valued as pigments for their vivid green, yellow, red and orange colours. The ruby takes its colour from chromium. Besides lustrous chrome plate, its alloys include a number of special hard steels.

| | | | | |
|---|---|---|---|---|
| 25 | MANGANESE | Mn | 54.938 | EARLY TRANS METALS |

From magnes, or magnet – its ore was first confused with magnetic iron ore; discovered 1774. Manganese, which gives steel a hard yet pliant quality, seems to play a similar role in animal bone: without it, bones grow spongier and break more easily. It activates many enzymes.

| | | | | |
|---|---|---|---|---|
| 26 | IRON | Fe | 55.847 | TRIADS |

From iren, its old English name; symbol Fe from its Latin name, ferrum; first utilised by prehistoric man. The fourth most abundant element and the cheapest metal, iron is the basic ingredient of all steel. Making up part of the compound haemoglobin, it carries oxygen in the bloodstream.

| | | | | |
|---|---|---|---|---|
| 27 | COBALT | Co | 58.933 | TRIADS |

From kobold, or evil spirit (its poisonous ores were once treacherous to mine); discovered 1735. For centuries cobalt's blue salts have given colour to porcelains, tiles and enamels. Its alloys go into making jet propulsion engines, and its radioactive isotope is used to treat cancer.

| | | | | |
|---|---|---|---|---|
| 28 | NICKEL | Ni | 58.7 | TRIADS |

From the German Kupfernickel, or false copper, a reddish ore contains nickel but no copper; discovered 1751. Its hard durable qualities have long made nickel popular for coins – the US 5-cent piece is 25% nickel, the rest copper. Nickel plate protects softer metals.

| | | | | |
|---|---|---|---|---|
| 29 | COPPER | Cu | 63.5 | LATE TRANS METALS |

From cuprum, derived from the ancient name of Cyprus, famed for its copper mines; known by early man. It and gold are the only two coloured metals. Alloyed in most gold jewellery and silverware, copper is mixed with zinc in brass, with tin in bronze. A 'copper' penny is bronze.

| Atomic Number | Elements | Symbol | Atomic Weight | Family |
|---|---|---|---|---|
| 30 | ZINC | Zn | 65.38 | LATE TRANS METALS |

Probably from zin, German for tin; discovered by the alchemist Paracelsus in the sixteenth century, though the zinc-copper alloy brass was known to the ancients. While not technically a coloured metal, zinc has a bluish cast. An excellent coating metal, it is used to line flashlight batteries.

| Atomic Number | Elements | Symbol | Atomic Weight | Family |
|---|---|---|---|---|
| 31 | GALLIUM | Ga | 69.72 | BORON/CARBON |

From Gallia, the old name for France; discovered 1875. A metal that melts in the hand, it is one of the few that expands as it freezes, as do non-metals and most gases. Its high boiling point – 1983°C – makes it ideal for recording temperatures that would vaporise a thermometer.

| Atomic Number | Elements | Symbol | Atomic Weight | Family |
|---|---|---|---|---|
| 32 | GERMANIUM | Ge | 72.59 | BORON/CARBON |

From Germany; discovered 1886. The first metal in the carbon family, germanium resembles the non-metal silicon. The first element used for transistors, it has brought about the replacement of large vacuum tubes with devices $1/400$ inch across.

| Atomic Number | Elements | Symbol | Atomic Weight | Family |
|---|---|---|---|---|
| 33 | ARSENIC | As | 74.933 | NITROGEN/OXYGEN |

From arsenikos, or male (the Greeks believed metals differed in sex); discovered about 1250. Best classed as a non-metal with a few metallic traits, arsenic is famed as a poison but some of its compounds are medicines. When heated it 'sublimes' – i.e the solid evaporates directly.

| Atomic Number | Elements | Symbol | Atomic Weight | Family |
|---|---|---|---|---|
| 34 | SELENIUM | Se | 78.96 | NITROGEN/OXYGEN |

From selene, or moon; discovered 1817; exists both as metal and non-metal. Unlike most electrical conductors, selenium varies in conductivity with variations in light. This 'photo-electric' trait makes it suitable for use in electric eyes, solar cells, television cameras and light meters.

| Atomic Number | Elements | Symbol | Atomic Weight | Family |
|---|---|---|---|---|
| 35 | BROMINE | Br | 79.9 | HALOGENS |

From bromos, or stench; discovered 1826; a red, caustic, fuming liquid, with a foul smell. Bromine is an effective disinfectant. Among its compounds are the bromides, used in nerve sedatives, and in petrol anti-knock compounds that make car engines run smoothly.

| Atomic Number | Elements | Symbol | Atomic Weight | Family |
|---|---|---|---|---|
| 36 | KRYPTON | Kr | 83.8 | NOBLE GASES |

From kryptos, or hidden; discovered in 1898. Radioactive krypton is used to keep tabs on Soviet nuclear production. Because this gas is a by-product of all nuclear reactors, the Russian share is found by subtracting the amount that comes from Western reactors from the total in the air.

| Atomic Number | Elements | Symbol | Atomic Weight | Family |
|---|---|---|---|---|
| 37 | RUBIDIUM | Rb | 85.47 | ALKALINE |

From rubidus, or red (the colour its salts impart to flames); discovered 1861. Used in electric eye-cells, also a potential space fuel. Like potassium, it is slightly radioactive, and has been used to locate brain tumours, as it collects in tumours but not in normal tissue.

| Atomic Number | Elements | Symbol | Atomic Weight | Family |
|---|---|---|---|---|
| 38 | STRONTIUM | Sr | 87.62 | ALKALINE |

From Strontian, Scotland; discovered 1790; a rare metal which is a sort of evil alter ego of life-supporting calcium. Radioactive strontium 90 is present in atomic fall-out. It is absorbed by bone tissue in place of calcium; enough of it destroys marrow and can cause cancer.

| | | | | |
|---|---|---|---|---|
| 39 | YTTRIUM | Y | 88.9 | EARLY TRANS METALS |

From the town of Ytterby, Sweden, where it was discovered in 1794; a scaly metal with an iron-grey sheen. Yttrium 90, a radioactive isotope, has a dramatic medical use in needles which have replaced the surgeon's knife in killing pain-transmitting nerves in the spinal cord.

| | | | | |
|---|---|---|---|---|
| 40 | ZIRCONIUM | Zr | 91.22 | EARLY TRANS METALS |

From zircon, the name of the semi-precious gemstone in which it was discovered in 1789. A metal unaffected by neutrons, zirconium serves as the inner lining of reactors in nuclear submarines and atomic power plants. It is also used as a building material for jets and rockets.

| | | | | |
|---|---|---|---|---|
| 41 | NIOBIUM | Nb | 92.906 | EARLY TRANS METALS |

From Niobe, daughter of the mythical Greek king Tantalus (niobium is found with tantalum); discovered 1801. Used in steel, atomic reactors, jet engines and rockets, it was known until 1950 as colombium, from Columbus – a poetic name for America, where its ore was first discovered.

| | | | | |
|---|---|---|---|---|
| 42 | MOLYBDENUM | Mo | 95.94 | EARLY TRANS METALS |

From molybdos, or lead – first found in what was originally thought to be lead-ore; discovered 1778. Fifth highest melting metal, it is used in boiler plate, rifle barrels and filaments. No vessel could be found in which to cast it until a special water-cooled crucible was devised in 1959.

| | | | | |
|---|---|---|---|---|
| 43 | TECHNETIUM | Tc | 98 | EARLY TRANS METALS |

From technetos, or artificial; produced 1937. The first man-made element, it was originally produced by the atomic bombardment of molybdenum. Later it was found among the fission products of uranium

| | | | | |
|---|---|---|---|---|
| 44 | RUTHENIUM | Ru | 101.07 | THE TRIADS |

From Ruthenia, Latin for Russia; discovered 1844. Pure ruthenium is too hard and brittle to machine. It makes an excellent 'hardener', however, when it is alloyed with platinum. But used in excess of 15%, ruthenium is ruinous, making the metals too hard to be worked.

| | | | | |
|---|---|---|---|---|
| 45 | RHODIUM | Rh | 102.91 | THE TRIADS |

From rhodon, or rose (its salts give a rosy solution); discovered 1803. Besides forming alloys, rhodium makes a lustrous, hard coating for other metals in such items as table silver and camera parts. A thin film of vaporised rhodium deposited on glass makes a very good mirror.

| Atomic Number | Elements | Symbol | Atomic Weight | Family |
|---|---|---|---|---|
| 46 | PALLADIUM | Pd | 106.4 | THE TRIADS |

After the asteroid Pallas; discovered 1803. Free from tarnish and corrosion-resistant, palladium is incorporated in contacts for telephone relays and high-grade surgical instruments. It is also used with gold, silver and other metals as a 'stiffener' in dental inlays and bridgework.

| Atomic Number | Elements | Symbol | Atomic Weight | Family |
|---|---|---|---|---|
| 47 | SILVER | Ag | 107.87 | LATE TRANS METALS |

From Old English seolfor, for silver; symbol Ag from its Latin name argentum; prehistoric; the best conductor of heat and electricity. Its salts are basic in photography; when silver bromide is exposed to light, it undergoes a chemical change which the developer then makes visible.

| Atomic Number | Elements | Symbol | Atomic Weight | Family |
|---|---|---|---|---|
| 48 | CADMIUM | Cd | 112.4 | LATE TRANS METALS |

From kadmia, or earth; discovered 1817. Cadmium occurs in nature with zinc. It makes excellent neutron-eating rods to slow down atomic chain reactions and finds use in nickel-cadmium batteries. Its bright sulphide makes the popular artist's pigment, cadmium yellow.

| Atomic Number | Elements | Symbol | Atomic Weight | Family |
|---|---|---|---|---|
| 49 | INDIUM | In | 114.82 | BORON/CARBON |

From the indigo blue it shows in a spectroscope; discovered 1863. A metal used in engine bearings, in transistors and as a 'glue' that adheres to glass, it is too scarce for large-scale use. But a minuscule, long-lived indium battery has been devised to power electronic wrist watches.

| Atomic Number | Elements | Symbol | Atomic Weight | Family |
|---|---|---|---|---|
| 50 | TIN | Sn | 118.69 | BORON/CARBON |

An Old English word; symbol Sn from stannum, Latin for tin. Prehistoric. Because it does not rust and resists other corrosion, tin has made canned food possible. A tin can is steel-coated with about 0.0005 of an inch of tin. Over 40,000 million cans are made each year.

| Atomic Number | Elements | Symbol | Atomic Weight | Family |
|---|---|---|---|---|
| 51 | ANTIMONY | Sb | 121.75 | NITROGEN/OXYGEN |

From antimonas, 'opposed to solitude' (it generally occurs mixed with other elements); symbol Sb from stibium, or mark (it was once used as eyebrow pencil). Discovered about 1450. Antimony is mixed with lead in batteries and goes into type metal and pewter alloys.

| Atomic Number | Elements | Symbol | Atomic Weight | Family |
|---|---|---|---|---|
| 52 | TELLURIUM | Te | 127.60 | NITROGEN/OXYGEN |

From tellus, the earth; discovered 1782. With both metallic and non-metallic traits, tellurium has several peculiarities. It is 'out of step' in the periodic table, having a lower atomic number but higher atomic weight than iodine. And inhaling its vapour results in garlicky breath.

| Atomic Number | Elements | Symbol | Atomic Weight | Family |
|---|---|---|---|---|
| 53 | IODINE | I | 126.90 | THE HALOGENS |

From iodes, or violet; discovered 1811. A blue-black solid which turns into a violet vapour when heated. Formerly prepared from seaweed, it is now produced from oil-well brines. Most table salt is now 'iodised' to supplement the human diet; an iodine deficiency causes thyroid trouble.

| Atomic Number | Elements | Symbol | Atomic Weight | Family |
|---|---|---|---|---|
| 54 | XENON | Xe | 131.3 | NOBLE GASES |

From xenos, or stranger; discovered 1898. The rarest gas in the atmosphere, xenon is used in specialised light sources such as the high-speed electronic flash bulbs used by photographers. In these, the high volatility of its electron structure produces an instant, intense light.

| 55 | CAESIUM | Cs | 132.91 | ALKALINE |
|---|---|---|---|---|

From caesius, or sky-blue (its salts turn flames blue); discovered 1860; the softest metal, liquid at warm room temperature, 28°C. Extremely reactive, it finds limited use in vacuum tubes and in atomic clocks so accurate that they vary no more than five seconds in ten generations.

| 56 | BARIUM | Ba | 137.3 | ALKALINE |
|---|---|---|---|---|

From barys, heavy or dense; discovered 1808. The white sulphate is drunk as a medical cocktail to outline the stomach and intestines for X-ray examination. Barium nitrate gives fireworks a green colour.

| 57 | LANTHANUM | La | 138.91 | EARLY TRANS METALS |
|---|---|---|---|---|

From lanthanein, to lie hidden; discovered 1839; highly reactive. Because it gives glass special light-bending, or 'refractive', properties, lanthanum is used in expensive camera lenses. Radioactive lanthanum has been tested for use in treating cancer.

| 58 | CERIUM | Ce | 140.12 | RARE EARTH METALS |
|---|---|---|---|---|

After the asteroid Ceres; discovered 1803; most abundant of the rare-earth elements. It is the chief ingredient (just under 50%) of misch-metal alloy. Cerium is used in alloys to make heat-resistant jet-engine parts; its oxide is a promising new petroleum-cracking catalyst.

| 59 | PRASEODYMIUM | Pr | 140.91 | RARE EARTH METALS |
|---|---|---|---|---|

From prasios didymos, or green twin (from its green salts); discovered 1885 when separated from its rare-earth twin neodymium. Together they are now used in making lenses for glassmaker's goggles because they filter out the yellow light present in glass blowing.

| 60 | NEODYMIUM | Nd | 144.24 | RARE EARTH METALS |
|---|---|---|---|---|

From neos didymium, or new twin; discovered 1885. In a pure form, it produces the only bright-purple glass known. In a cruder state, it is used to take colour out of glass and to make special glass that transmits the tanning rays of the sun but not the unwanted infra-red heat rays.

| 61 | PROMETHIUM | Pm | 145 | RARE EARTH METALS |
|---|---|---|---|---|

After Prometheus; discovered 1947; the only rare earth that has never been found in nature. Produced in nuclear reactors, radioactive promethium in an 'atomic battery' no bigger than a drawing pin powers guided-missile instruments, watches and radios.

| Atomic Number | Elements | Symbol | Atomic Weight | Family |
|---|---|---|---|---|
| 62 | SAMARIUM | Sm | 150.36 | RARE EARTH METALS |

From the mineral samarskite, named after a Russian mine official, Colonel V.E. Samarsky; discovered 1879. Calcium chloride crystals treated with samarium have been employed in lasers – devices for producing beams of light intense enough to burn metal or bounce off the moon.

| | | | | |
|---|---|---|---|---|
| 63 | EUROPIUM | Eu | 151.96 | RARE EARTH METALS |

From Europe; discovered 1896. Most reactive rare earth. The metal had virtually no practical use until the atomic age. But atom for atom, europium can absorb more neutrons than any other element, making it valuable in control rods for nuclear reactors.

| | | | | |
|---|---|---|---|---|
| 64 | GADOLINIUM | Gd | 157.25 | RARE EARTH METALS |

From the mineral gadolinite, named after a Finnish chemist; discovered 1880. Falling in the middle of the rare-earth series, gadolinium divides the lighter metals, which tend to impart pliant qualities to alloys, from the heavier metals, used mostly as strengthening agents.

| | | | | |
|---|---|---|---|---|
| 65 | TERBIUM | Tb | 158.9 | RARE EARTH METALS |

From Ytterby, Sweden; discovered 1843; named after the town that also gave its name to three other elements; the rare earths ytterbium and erbium and the transition metal yttrium. Like all rare earths, terbium in an impure state is pyrophoric – i.e. it bursts into flame when heated.

| | | | | |
|---|---|---|---|---|
| 66 | DYSPROSIUM | Dy | 162.50 | RARE EARTH METALS |

From dysprositos, or hard to get at; discovered 1886. Dysprosium's chief practical use is in nuclear reactors, where it serves as a nuclear 'poison' – i.e. it is employed as a neutron-eating material to keep the neutron-spawning atomic chain reaction from getting out of hand.

| | | | | |
|---|---|---|---|---|
| 67 | HOLMIUM | Ho | 164.93 | RARE EARTH METALS |

From Holmia, Latin name for Stockholm; discovered 1879. Like dysprosium, holmium is a metal which can absorb fission-bred neutrons. It is used in nuclear reactors as a burnable poison – i.e. one that burns up while it is keeping a chain reaction from running out of control.

| | | | | |
|---|---|---|---|---|
| 68 | ERBIUM | Er | 167.26 | RARE EARTH METALS |

From Ytterby, Sweden; discovered 1843. Used in ceramics as erbium oxide to produce a pink glaze. Erbium, holmium and dysprosium are almost identical in terms of their chemical and physical properties. They vary from each other only by one electron in their third inner orbit.

| | | | | |
|---|---|---|---|---|
| 69 | THULIUM | Tm | 168.93 | RARE EARTH METALS |

From Thule, or Northland; discovered 1879. When irradiated in a nuclear reactor, thulium produces an isotope that gives off X-rays. A 'button' of this isotope is used to make a lightweight, portable X-ray machine for medical use. The 'hot' thulium is replaced every few months.

| Atomic Number | Elements | Symbol | Atomic Weight | Family |
|---|---|---|---|---|
| 70 | YTTERBIUM | Yb | 173.04 | RARE EARTH METALS |

From Ytterby, Sweden; discovered 1907. This element is still little more than a laboratory curiosity. Along with the other rare earths, it recently turned up in Russia in a mineral called gagarinite after the first astronaut. Easily oxidised.

| Atomic Number | Elements | Symbol | Atomic Weight | Family |
|---|---|---|---|---|
| 71 | LUTETIUM | Lu | 174.97 | RARE EARTH METALS |

From Lutetia, the ancient name for Paris; discovered 1907; heaviest of the rare earths. Although rare-earth alloys such as misch metal are cheap, pure lutetium is highly expensive. With many of its chemical and physical properties unknown, it has no practical value.

| Atomic Number | Elements | Symbol | Atomic Weight | Family |
|---|---|---|---|---|
| 72 | HAFNIUM | Hf | 178.49 | EARLY TRANS METALS |

From Hafnia, the Latin name for Copenhagen; discovered 1923. A 'wonder metal' of the atomic age, hafnium has a great appetite for neutrons. Thus it goes into neutron-absorbing reactor control rods which slow down nuclear chain reactions and also quench atomic 'fires'.

| Atomic Number | Elements | Symbol | Atomic Weight | Family |
|---|---|---|---|---|
| 73 | TANTALUM | Ta | 180.95 | EARLY TRANS METALS |

From King Tantalus of Greek myth; discovered 1802. Almost impervious to corrosion, tantalum is vital in surgical repairs of the human body; it can replace bone (for example in skull plates); as foil or wire it connects torn nerves; as woven gauze it binds up abdominal muscles.

| Atomic Number | Elements | Symbol | Atomic Weight | Family |
|---|---|---|---|---|
| 74 | TUNGSTEN | W | 183.85 | EARLY TRANS METALS |

From Swedish tungsten, or heavy stone; symbol W from its German name wolfram; discovered 1783. The highest melting of metals at 3410°C – tungsten in filaments withstands intense heat in light bulbs. New tungsten-tipped 'painless' dental drills spin at ultra-high speed.

| Atomic Number | Elements | Symbol | Atomic Weight | Family |
|---|---|---|---|---|
| 75 | RHENIUM | Re | 186.2 | EARLY TRANS METALS |

From the Rhine provinces of Germany; discovered 1925. Rhenium is the ninth scarcest element and has the second highest melting point. It is used in 'thermocouples' (electric thermometers for measuring high temperatures) and in the contact points of electrical switches.

| Atomic Number | Elements | Symbol | Atomic Weight | Family |
|---|---|---|---|---|
| 76 | OSMIUM | Os | 190.2 | THE TRIADS |

From osme, or odour; discovered 1804. A metal with a pungent smell, it is used to produce alloys of extreme hardness. Pen tips and 'lifetime' gramophone needles are 60% osmium. It is the densest metal known: a brick-sized chunk of osmium weighs about 56 pounds.

| Atomic Number | Elements | Symbol | Atomic Weight | Family |
|---|---|---|---|---|
| 77 | IRIDIUM | Ir | 192.2 | THE TRIADS |

From iris, or rainbow, so named for its colourful salts; discovered 1804. Very hard and hence extremely difficult to work, iridium hardens other metals. Its alloys make bars used as standard weights and measures. The international 'standard metre' is platinum-iridium.

| Atomic Number | Elements | Symbol | Atomic Weight | Family |
|---|---|---|---|---|
| 78 | PLATINUM | Pt | 195.08 | THE TRIADS |

From platina, or little silver; discovered in the sixteenth century. Found in nuggets of up to 21 pounds, it is used not only in weights and measures but also in catalysts, delicate instruments and electrical equipment. Its cost (more than gold) has demanded a hallmark for platinum jewellery.

| | | | | |
|---|---|---|---|---|
| 79 | GOLD | Au | 196.97 | LATE TRANS METALS |

From the Old English word geolo, or yellow; symbol Au from its Latin name aurum; prehistoric; the most malleable metal. Man's lust for gold has been a delusion, for he has pursued little more than a yellow gleam. Until the advent of computer components, it could not be used for much besides money, jewellery and dental work.

| | | | | |
|---|---|---|---|---|
| 80 | MERCURY | Hg | 200.59 | LATE TRANS METALS |

From the planet Mercury; symbol Hg from hydrargyrum, or liquid silver; prehistoric. It appears in the glass tubing of thermometers and barometers; it also finds use in 'silver' dental inlays and in silent electric switches. Vaporised mercury fills modern blue-hued street lights.

| | | | | |
|---|---|---|---|---|
| 81 | THALLIUM | Tl | 204.38 | BORON/CARBON |

From thallos, or a young shoot – its spectrum is a bright-green line; discovered 1861. Its chief use is in thallium sulphate – a deadly rat poison. Odourless and tasteless, it is mixed with starch, sugar, glycerine and water to make an inviting if ominous 'treat' for household rodents.

| | | | | |
|---|---|---|---|---|
| 82 | LEAD | Pb | 207.2 | BORON/CARBON |

From Old English lead; symbol Pb from its Latin name, plumbum, also the origin of plumber. Prehistoric. Enormously durable, lead has been the backbone of plumbing for centuries. Lead pipes once used to drain the baths of ancient Rome have been uncovered still in working order.

| | | | | |
|---|---|---|---|---|
| 83 | BISMUTH | Bi | 208.98 | NITROGEN/OXYGEN |

From the German *wismuth*, or white mass; discovered 1450. The most metallic member of its family, bismuth melts at 271°C but forms alloys that melt at as low as 47°C. These find wide application in electric fuses, solders and in automatic fire-sprinkler systems.

| | | | | |
|---|---|---|---|---|
| 84 | POLONIUM | Po | 209 | NITROGEN/OXYGEN |

After Poland; found in 1898 by Pierre and Marie Curie in pitchblende. The scarcest natural element, it was the first to be discovered by the Curies. It is sold as an alpha-particle source for scientific use.

| | | | | |
|---|---|---|---|---|
| 85 | ASTATINE | At | 210 | THE HALOGENS |

From astatos, or unstable; discovered 1940. Astatine, prepared by bombarding bismuth atoms with helium nuclei, is radioactive and has a maximum half-life of 83 hours. Its detection is recorded in the notebook of one of its discoverers, American physicist D.R. Corson.

| Atomic Number | Elements | Symbol | Atomic Weight | Family |
|---|---|---|---|---|
| 86 | RADON | Rn | 222 | NOBLE GASES |

From radium; discovered 1900. Heaviest gaseous element, it is emitted by radium and is itself radioactive; it decays into radioactive polonium and alpha rays. This radiation makes radon useful in cancer therapy; gold needles filled with the gas are implanted into the diseased tissue.

| | | | | |
|---|---|---|---|---|
| 87 | FRANCIUM | Fr | 223 | ALKALINE |

From France; discovered 1939. A short-lived product of the decay of actinium, francium has never actually been seen. A graph identifies francium by its radiation in the notebook of its discoverer, Marguerite Perey, a one-time assistant to Marie Curie.

| | | | | |
|---|---|---|---|---|
| 88 | RADIUM | Ra | 226 | ALKALINE |

From radius, or ray; discovered 1898 by Pierre and Marie Curie; sixth rarest of the elements. Radium bromide mixed with zinc sulphide is used in luminous watch dials. The radium gives off dangerous radiation which causes the zinc sulphide to glow.

| | | | | |
|---|---|---|---|---|
| 89 | ACTINIUM | Ac | 227 | ACTINIDE |

From aktinos, or ray; discovered 1899. Second rarest of the elements. Found in pitchblende. With a half-life of 22 years, actinium decomposes into francium and helium.

| | | | | |
|---|---|---|---|---|
| 90 | THORIUM | Th | 232.04 | ACTINIDE |

From Thor, Scandinavian war god; discovered 1828. Thorium can be used instead of scarce uranium as a reactor fuel because it is readily converted into uranium. Almost as abundant as lead, earthly thorium stores more energy than all uranium, coal, oil and other fuels combined.

| | | | | |
|---|---|---|---|---|
| 91 | PROTACTINIUM | Pa | 231 | ACTINIDE |

From protos, or first; it is the parent of actinium, which is formed by its radioactive decay; discovered 1917. Third rarest of the elements, it can be prepared by modern chemical techniques from thorium or uranium.

| | | | | |
|---|---|---|---|---|
| 92 | URANIUM | U | 238.03 | ACTINIDE |

After the planet Uranus; discovered 1789; the heaviest atom among the natural elements. Its most common form has a half-life of 4500 million years. In a nuclear reactor, it generates neutrons to keep the chain reaction going.

| | | | | |
|---|---|---|---|---|
| 93 | NEPTUNIUM | Np | 237 | ACTINIDE |

After Neptune, the planet beyond Uranus; discovered 1940. Detected first in invisible, unweighable amounts, neptunium was the first 'synthetic' element made from uranium. Traces of it turn up in uranium ores, produced by stray neutrons from uranium's decay.

| Atomic Number | Elements | Symbol | Atomic Weight | Family |
|---|---|---|---|---|
| 94 | PLUTONIUM | Pu | 244 | ACTINIDE |

After Pluto, the planet beyond Neptune; discovered 1940. Plutonium was used, instead of uranium, in several of the first atomic bombs. In one of the codes of wartime physicists, plutonium was referred to as 'copper'; copper itself had to be renamed 'honest-to-God copper'.

| 95 | AMERICIUM | Am | 243 | ACTINIDE |
|---|---|---|---|---|

Named after the Americas, by analogy with the rare earth europium; discovered 1944. Americium is produced by bombarding plutonium with neutrons. It has been made in gramme quantities which, in the world of such elements, is virtually a superabundance.

| 96 | CURIUM | Cm | 247 | ACTINIDE |
|---|---|---|---|---|

In honour of Pierre and Marie Curie, pioneers in the field of radioactivity; discovered 1944. Curium, with a half-life of 19 years, is a decay product of americium. Curium hydroxide is the first known curium compound.

| 97 | BERKELIUM | Bk | 247 | ACTINIDE |
|---|---|---|---|---|

After Berkeley, the home of the University of California, whose scientists have detected all 11 of the transuranium elements; discovered 1949. Many infinitesimal samples of berkelium have been prepared.

| 98 | CALIFORNIUM | Cf | 251 | ACTINIDE |
|---|---|---|---|---|

After the State and University of California; discovered 1950. Not until 1960 did californium exist in visible amounts.

| 99 | EINSTEINIUM | Es | 252 | ACTINIDE |
|---|---|---|---|---|

After Albert Einstein; discovered 1952. It was first detected in the debris from the 1952 H-bomb explosion at Eniwetok in the Pacific after tons of radioactive coral from atolls in the blast area were sifted and examined. The element was later made in a nuclear reactor.

| 100 | FERMIUM | Fm | 257 | ACTINIDE |
|---|---|---|---|---|

After Enrico Fermi; discovered 1953. Ferminium, like einsteinium, was first isolated from the debris of the 1952 H-bomb test, having been produced from the fission of uranium. Because of its short lifespan, scientists doubt that enough fermium will ever be obtained to be weighed.

| 101 | MENDELEVIUM | Md | 258 | ACTINIDE |
|---|---|---|---|---|

After Dmitri Mendeleyev, who devised the periodic table; discovered in 1955. Bombarding the scantest unweighable quantities of einsteinium with helium nuclei, scientists identified mendelevium from the barest shred of evidence – one to three atoms per bombardment.

| 102 | NOBELIUM | No | 259 | ACTINIDE |
|---|---|---|---|---|

After Alfred Nobel. A 1957 claim of discovery is disputed, but nobelium was positively identified in 1958 by a team of University of California scientists. Observations were not made on nobelium itself but on atoms of fermium 250 – 'daughter atoms' produced by nobelium's decay.

| Atomic Number | Elements | Symbol | Atomic Weight | Family |
|---|---|---|---|---|
| 103 | LAWRENCIUM | Lr | 260 | ACTINIDE |

After Ernest O Lawrence. Discovered in 1961 at Lawrence Radiation Laboratories, lawrencium was made by bombardment of californium with boron in a chamber fitted with a copper conveyor; the new atoms, one at a time, were carried to a radiation detector for identification.

| Atomic Number | Elements | Symbol | Atomic Weight | Family |
|---|---|---|---|---|
| 104 | UNNILQUADIUM | Unq | 261 | ACTINIDE |

Originally named after Lord Ernest Rutherford, was produced in 1969 at Lawrence Radiation Laboratory by bombardment of californium with carbon nuclei. Soviet scientists had earlier announced the discovery of element 104, but this was not accepted internationally.

| Atomic Number | Elements | Symbol | Atomic Weight | Family |
|---|---|---|---|---|
| 105 | UNNIPENTIUM | Unp | 262 | ACTINIDE |

Originally named after Otto Hahn of Germany, one of the discoverers of uranium fission. It was synthesised in 1970 by bombardment of californium with nitrogen nuclei. The name of this element was recently confirmed by the International Union of Pure and Applied Chemistry.

## Onword

Once you have memorised the basic elements, and understood their properties, your brain is set for one of the most fascinating adventures imaginable!

# Solar System <sup>The</sup> **19**

This chapter encourages you to expand on this already expanding area of your knowledge, and to continue your journey . . .

During the last five centuries, mankind has discovered, with accelerating knowledge and fascination, that the neighbouring Planets (wanderers) of our Solar System are not simply barren rocks. Each is an astonishingly different world, with its own part to play in our search for information about our own origins.

Our Solar System's Planets include one with a surface as hot as a furnace; one with a thick blanket of clouds that veils her secrets from us and through which we are just beginning to probe; one with a surface like the deserts of Australia, and which may well sustain life; one that is bigger than all the others put together, and which has a gigantic red eye which is still not fully explained, that would swallow the Earth; one with giant rings around it and strange moons which may harbour life; one covered by vast oceans of liquid gas and a core that resembles Earth; and all the Planets are being explored as you read this book.

At this point in history, our Solar System is to us as the rest of the world was to the first European explorers: the great unknown, the arena for our next great explorations and adventures, and the environment which many of our children, grandchildren and great-grandchildren will call home.

Thus, a knowledge of our Solar System will give you your first intellectual grappling hooks into a knowledge and understanding of the universe. In so doing, it will give you a greater understanding of and perspective on your place in the scheme of all things, and will make you a part of two of man's greatest intellectual voyages: the journeys to discover the secrets of the brain and the secrets of the universe.

In this particular 'Memory Area', you are *already* an embryonic expert, for you have mastered the initial exercise and attendant explanation on pages 19–20 of chapter 3.

Asteroids are huge chunks of rock, orbiting the sun between Mars and Jupiter. They are minor Planets. There may be as many as 40,000 of them.

# THE SOLAR SYSTEM

| | Mercury | Venus | Earth | Mars | Jupiter | Saturn | Uranus | Neptune | Pluto |
|---|---|---|---|---|---|---|---|---|---|
| Mean Distance from Sun (millions of miles) | 36.0 | 67.1 | 92.9 | 141.5 | 483.4 | 886.7 | 1782.7 | 2794.3 | 3666.1 |
| Diameter (equatorial) (miles) | 3031 | 7521 | 7926 | 4221 | 88,734 | 74,566 | 31,566 | 30,199 | 1864 |
| Mass (Earth = 1) | 0.055 | 0.814 | 1.000 | 0.107 | 317.8 | 95.16 | 14.55 | 17.23 | 0.0026(?) |
| Density (Water = 1) | 5.43 | 5.24 | 5.52 | 3.93 | 1.33 | 0.71 | 1.31 | 1.77 | 1.1 |
| Volume (Earth = 1) | 0.06 | 0.86 | 1.00 | 0.15 | 1.323 | 752 | 64 | 54 | 0.01 |
| Revolution around Sun | 88.0 days | 224.7 days | 365.26 days | 687.0 days | 11.86 yrs | 29.46 yrs | 84.01 yrs | 164.8 yrs | 247.7 yrs |
| Rotation Period (days) | 58.65 | 243.0 | 0.9973 | 1.0260 | 0.410 | 0.427 | 0.45 | 0.67 | 6.3867 |
| Mean Orbital Speed (miles per second) | 29.8 | 21.7 | 18.6 | 14.9 | 8.0 | 6.0 | 4.2 | 3.3 | 2.9 |
| Inclination of Orbit (to Earth's Orbital Plane) | 7.0 | 3.4 | 0.0 | 1.8 | 1.3 | 2.5 | 0.8 | 1.8 | 17.2 |
| Gravity (Earth = 1) | 0.38 | 0.90 | 1.00 | 0.38 | 2.53 | 1.07 | 0.92 | 1.19 | 0.05(?) |

| Moons | Mercury | Venus | Earth | Mars | Jupiter | Saturn | Uranus | Neptune | Pluto |
|---|---|---|---|---|---|---|---|---|---|
| | – | – | Moon | Phobos | Io | Mimas | Ariel | Triton | Charon |
| | | | | Deimos | Europa | Enceladus | Umbriel | Nereid | |
| | | | | | Ganymede | Tethys | Titania | Naiad | |
| | | | | | Callisto | Dione | Oberon | Thalassa | |
| | | | | | Leda | Rhea | Miranda | Despina | |
| | | | | | Amalthea | Titan | Cordelia | Galatea | |
| | | | | | Himalia | Hyperion | Ophelia | Larissa | |
| | | | | | Elara | Iapetus | Bianca | Proteus | |
| | | | | | Pasiphae | Phoebe | Cressida | | |
| | | | | | Sinope | Janus | Desdemona | | |
| | | | | | Lysithea | Epimetheus | Juliet | | |
| | | | | | Carme | Helene | Portia | | |
| | | | | | Ananke | Telesto | Rosalind | | |
| | | | | | Thebe | Calypso | Belinda | | |
| | | | | | Adrastea | Atlas | Puck | | |
| | | | | | Metis | Prometheus | Caliban | | |
| | | | | | | Pandora | Sycorax | | |
| | | | | | | Pan | | | |

# Memorising Your Life:
## Your Memory and Your Future

**20**

> If you wish to remember the major elements of your past, present and future life, SEM$^3$ enables you to do so with ease.

Allow one Key Memory Word for each month. In so doing, it is possible, by adding a few major items for the month on a Link System, to remember eight years within 100 Key Image Words in the Self-Enhancing Master Memory Matrix.

The memorisation of your life can be made easier and more enjoyable by using a diary/self-management system such as the Universal Personal Organiser (UPO) (*available from the Buzan Organization, see page 192*). Such a system makes use of all the Memory Principles and Techniques, organises the year, months and days in such a way as to enable you to use all your cortical and memory skills, and allows you to record, using Mind Maps and the Memory Principles, all those important aspects of your life that you consider memorable.

The dream of memorising an entire life has been one of the 'mental holy grails' of the human race. You will already have read in chapter 7 about the astonishing memory of Irenio Funes, whose feats you might have thought (before reading this book) utterly impossible. Now you know such feats are achievable, and you also know they are well worth achieving. As Jean-Jacques Rousseau, the famous French writer, philosopher and poet, wrote in 1770:

*En écrivant mes souvenirs je me rappelerai le temps passé,
qui doublera pour ainsi dire mon existence.*

**(In writing my memoirs I recall the past times which
will double, so to speak, my existence.)**

SEM$^3$ certainly allows you, in grasping this opportunity, to double
your existence. It will also allow you to double your appreciation
and *enjoyment* of that existence. Take the opportunity – it is now
easily within your grasp.

### Conclusion – Your Future

Now that you have completed your first reading of *Master
Your Memory*, you are well on the way to providing the essential
'software' for the incredible 'hardware' of your super-
biocomputer brain.

This is a task that will give you greater mental power and
greater joy for the remainder of your life.

Since the invention of SEM$^3$, an increasing number of people
have become involved in networks and clubs designed to provide
companions and help on this Fantastic Voyage.

On pages 191–2 there is information on these organisations if
you wish to continue your journey . . .

Also consider entering the World Memory Championships and
exercising your memory in 'Memory Gymnasiums'. The following
websites will give you giant playgrounds in which to exercise your
Memory Muscle:

www.buzanworld.com

It has been a delight sharing memory with you; I similarly look
forward to sharing *future* memories!

# Recommended Reading

**Atkinson, Richard C.,** and **Shiffrin, Richard M.** 'The Control of Short-term Memory.' *Scientific American.* August 1971.

**Baddeley, Alan D.** *The Psychology of Memory.* New York: Harper & Row, 1976.

**Borges, Jorge L.,** *Fictions* (especially 'Funes, the Memorious'). London: J. Calder, 1985.

**Brown, Mark.** *Memory Matters.* Newton Abbot: David & Charles,1977.

**Buzan, Tony.** The Mind Set: *Use Your Head, Use Your Memory, The Speed Reading Book* and *The Mind Map Book.* All London: BBC Worldwide, 2000.

**Buzan, Tony.** *WH Smith GCSE Revision Guides* (60).

**Buzan, Tony.** *Head First, The Power of Creative Intelligence, The Power of Spiritual Intelligence, The Power of Social Intelligence, The Power of Verbal Intelligence, Head Strong, How to Mind Map.* All London: Harper Collins, 2002.

**Gelb, Michael J.** *How to Think Like Leonardo da Vinci.* New York: Delacorte Press, 1998.

**Haber, Ralph N.** 'How We Remember What We See.' *Scientific American,* May 1970.

**Hunt, E.,** and **Love, T.** 'How Good Can Memory Be?' In *Coding Processes in Human Memory,* pp. 237–60, edited by A.W. Melton and E. Martin, Washington, DC: Winston, Wiley, 1972, op.

**Hunter, I.M.L.,** 'An Exceptional Memory', *British Journal of Psychology* **68**, 155–64, 1977.

**Luria, A.R.** *The Mind of a Mnemonist.* Cambridge, Mass: Harvard University Press, 1987.

**North, Vanda,** with **Buzan, Tony.** *Get Ahead.* UK: Buzan Centres Ltd, 1991.

**Penry, J.** *Looking at Faces and Remembering Them. A Guide to Facial Identification.* London: Elek Books, 1971, op.

**Ruger, H.A.,** and **Bussenius, C. E.** *Memory.* New York: Teachers College Press, 1913 (OP).

**Stratton, George M.** 'The Mnemonic Feat of the "Shass Pollak".' *Physiological Review* **24**, 244–7.

**Thomas, E.J.** 'The Variation of Memory with Time for Information Appearing During a Lecture.' *Studies in Adult Education,* 57–62, April 1972.

**Wagner, D.** 'Memories of Morocco: the influence of age, schooling and environment on memory,' *Cognitive Psychology* **10**, 1–28, 1978.

**Yates, F.A.** *The Art of Memory.* London: Routledge & Kegan Paul, 1966; Ark, 1984.

# Index

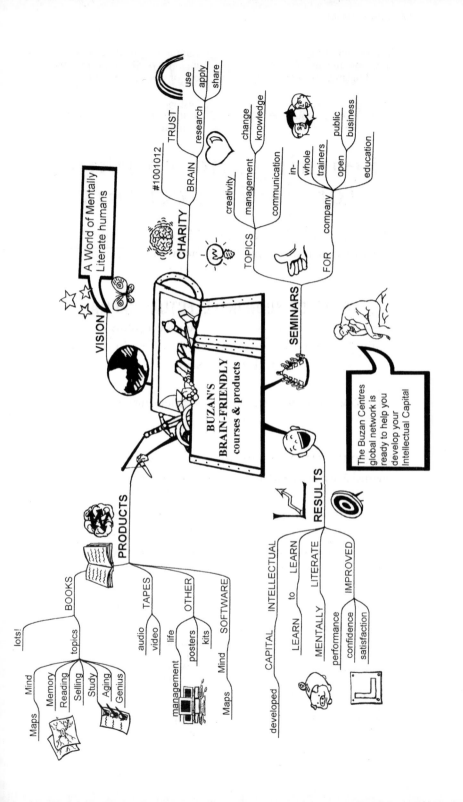

HAVERING COLLEGE OF F & H E

47919

# BUZAN CENTRES

This book is due for return on or before the last date shown below.

1 9 FEB 2007

1 0 NOV 2008

1 8 NOV 2008

2 4 NOV 2009

-6 FEB 2012

1 6 SEP 2011

WITHDRAWN

he
.

For enquiries or renewal at
Quarles LRC
Tel: 01708 455011 – Extension 4009